I Lied,
There's More

*WITH EMPHASIS
ON FRIENDSHIP*

Tom McCollough

iUniverse LLC
Bloomington

I Lied, There's More
with emphasis on friendship

iUniverse books may be ordered through booksellers or by contacting:

iUniverse LLC
1663 Liberty Drive
Bloomington, IN 47403
www.iuniverse.com
1-800-Authors (1-800-288-4677)

ISBN: 978-1-4759-9870-2 (sc)
ISBN: 978-1-4759-9871-9 (ebk)

Library of Congress Control Number: 2013912653

Printed in the United States of America

iUniverse rev. date: 07/16/2013

for Donn and Sharon

For good times and bad times
I'll be on your side forevermore.
That's what friends are for.
—Burt Bacharach

Contents

PREFACE

I lied—there's more. I didn't intend to publish another book of VIN YETS but two things happened. Publishing costs money, but I have decided it is not likely I can take it with me, so I might as well spend some before the postal rates go up again.

I go to our writers group every month and I never want to go empty-handed, so I keep writing for their benefit. The friendly members have become very close as we continue to explain ourselves to one another.

But perhaps the most important reason for this book is that I have become even more interested in the writing process, from the idea, to a first draft, through the editing phase. Editing becomes critical to evolve clarity and to try to say what you mean as simply as possible. First drafts contain a lot of mush that needs cooking and stirring to turn words from conversation into writing. I enjoy doing it.

I have dedicated this book to Sharon Sachs and Donn Vickers. When they married in Moffat, Scotland, I was the best man, and my wife Marian was Sharon's maid of honor. When we celebrated our fiftieth wedding anniversary at Yosemite, Donn and Sharon were honored guests, although Sharon fell and broke her ankle. (That

is, we have shared both good and bad times together.)
Friendship, like parenthood, is a subtle relationship that
surpasses reason. It is a treasure.

No more promises about the future. A book a year?
Mother lived until she was ninety. That would mean six
more books.

Oh my!

FRIENDS

How do you define a friend? Typically a friend is a non-family member with whom you have spent a lot of time sharing experiences and who is supportive, nonjudgmental, and a person you want to spend time with. Friendships start in childhood, usually with a person your age and sex with whom you play.

My first memorable friend was Barney Ruckdershel. He lived across the alley. We became friends about the time we started kindergarten. We visited nearly every day. He had a small closet in his bedroom filled with toys, including an Erector Set, Lincoln Logs, and both a Raggedy Ann and a Raggedy Andy doll that were always present for fantasy and imagination. We were inseparable. One summer Barney's family took me to Lake Wallenpaupack for their family vacation. On other occasions, we would travel to the Jersey Shore for a day at the beach. In 1939 my family moved to the suburbs, and I never saw Barney again.

In the new neighborhood, I made a new friend, Tom Good. Tom was blind at birth, and he was three or four years older than I was. Tom attended the blind school nearby and learned to play the piano almost professionally. I became one of his readers and gradually a close friend.

His family supported his musical inclinations and bought him shelves of 78 RPM classical phonograph records. We listened to "The Moldau" by Smetena dozens of times.

But Tom was important for a more special reason. He was sleeping with a young girl at the boarding school for the blind. We would gather a small group of friends, walk to a nearby pond, sit on a stone bridge, and Tom would share *all* the minute details of his active sex life. We were spellbound; sex was never discussed at home. Because of Tom, I learned all about the birds and bees.

Throughout life, friends are like the tides. They ebb and flow with the circumstances of life. Who do you eat lunch with? Who is assigned to your class roll? Who do you sing with in the choir? Who do you work with at the office? Friends may be casual or more—much more. In the army, you share weekend passes with Roy McLeese. In college you bus trays in the summer with Fred in Swampscott, Massachusetts. Sometimes you may become overly enmeshed with friends: a messy marriage separation and reconciliation, a friend's illness, a special occasion when you become one of the planners. Various shades of involvement mean different levels of intensity and adherence to friends.

The marines look for a few good men. I have a few good friends, ones I can be candidly honest with, ones I can share the ups and downs of life with without embarrassment or stress, ones who understand that life is messy and unpredictable. The word "few" is important, at best a handful, and what a treasure they are. It would be a breach of intimacy to name all of them or share our secrets.

But you know who you are, don't you?

A KINDLED FRIENDSHIP

Recently Donn and Sharon flew from Ohio to visit for a few days. They are old friends with whom we have shared many experiences: a career shift, international travel, conversations while naked in our hot tub, buying and enjoying art and artists, and hundreds of others.

When does friendship become something more? Something more intimate, more intertwined, with an unspoken understanding of psyches, so close that lives are changed? That is exactly what has happened to Marian and me since we have known Donn and Sharon.

Their visit lasted four days and had at least thirty-seven highlights, maybe more. The first was just having them here, flooding us with memories of mostly wonderful times together, with a few exceptions. Once in Nova Scotia, Donn choked on an after-dinner mint, started gasping, and turned scarlet. We thought he was teasing us—he often pulled pranks—but something was seriously wrong. I grabbed and squeezed him with the Heimlich maneuver, and he started breathing again. Those are memories you cannot forget.

In a previous VIN YET I rued having sold at auction a George Bellows lithograph of a nude drawn sometime about 1924. I purchased it in the mid-1970s at the Columbus Museum of Art. (Bellows was raised in Columbus, and the museum was selling off some of their surplus holdings.)

Donn recalled that I missed the art and asked an art gallery operator to look for one. One turned up—one of thirty-nine in the world. Donn arrived in Saratoga with it as a gift, and I nearly cried. Is that friendship or what? What I paid a pittance for is now worth thousands. While Donn was here, we went to the frame store, selected a frame that we both approved, and I started imaging where I would hang it.

Sharon too is thoughtful. She had noted that we enjoyed a spice cake called "poor man's bread," a recipe from World War I when there were few eggs or milk. She and Marian put the cake together early one morning, and the apartment bloomed with the odor of aromatic spices. I am eating a large piece as I write this.

Marian and Sharon share the same birthday, August 6, although Sharon is twenty years younger. On their birthdays, we were often able to do something special: travel, eat a good meal, exchange gifts, etc. We added their ages together each year, and when they were one hundred, we were in Nova Scotia.

For many years we spent quiet New Year's Eves together. Sometimes we would make it to midnight, sometimes not. Donn was active in leadership roles in the Ohio arts community and usually had a suggestion for something unique to do. One New Year's Eve, we read together favorite passages from books we loved. I read aloud some of the last sentences from James Joyce's *Dubliners,* which has some of the most beautiful sentences ever written in English language.

Donn was the founder and first director of the Thurber House Museum in Columbus. When we sold our farm, the literary director of the Thurber House bought the property, and he still lives and writes books there. Thurber's daughter, Rosie, helped Donn with the museum project and came often to Columbus for events. One summer we, including Rosie, went to Tuscany for a vacation, renting one of those four-hundred-year-old stone farmhouses overlooking the vineyards from which Chianti is made.

I could write a book about the nature of our friendship with Donn and Sharon, the experiences we have shared, and the depth of what it has all meant.

Friendship is a fluffy kitten. No, Donn is allergic to cats. Friendship is a fluffy puppy.

NORM:
MORE THAN A FRIEND

Norm McCray died in his sleep. He had been fishing the day before, went to bed, and was dead before dawn—a good way to go if you must go, and typical of Normie. He was a tease, delighted in playing tricks on people, and was unpredictable. People never knew whether he was kidding or serious.

Norm was a retired high school shop teacher who sometimes taught student driving. Once doing yard duty at the school, he caught a young fellow smoking. The student cupped the cigarette in his fist. Instead of saying anything, Norm went over and struck up a long conversation with the youngster, knowing full well that the cigarette was burning in his hand.

Norm was a master carpenter who constructed our old barn into a luxurious garage, guest house, office, and art gallery. At times he would be a master plumber, then a master electrician, then an avid gardener, then a raconteur, then a hunter and fisherman. He was by definition a jack of all trades. He was always on the move. In spring he would leave bags of freshly cut asparagus hanging from your front door, and in summer fresh lettuce and tomatoes, or eggplant and zucchini. He stopped growing sweet corn because Ohio summer thunderstorms would blow it over just as it was ready to pick. Instead, he relied on the Amish sweet corn grown nearby. Few people knew that he grew fanciful orchids in his basement under artificial lights.

Norm had a weight problem. His belly would protrude over his jeans and suspenders. He would go on a salad diet for a few months, lose thirty pounds, look great, and gain it all back.

As Marian and I became more infirm, he became our chauffeur. He drove us to Sanibel each year. We would fly him home after the drive and then back again to pick us up. When we moved to California, he drove us there from Florida. He loved to drive. He never charged us anything. He enjoyed the sightseeing, the food, and the long conversations we had in the car. In Florida we plied him with shrimp and grouper, and he remained happy to continue the service. He hated it when I turned on classical music when driving, so I bought a DVD player with earphones.

We've been to the Grand Canyon, Sea Ranch in California, Savannah, Opryland, and dozens of other intriguing places with Norm. He was an intimate part of our life. When we moved to California, he would call every month or so just to say hello, tell us a little gossip about Glenford, or report on the weather and his family, explaining what his wife, Arlene, had cooked for supper the night before.

And now he has gone, overnight.

If there is a heaven and Norm is there, he is already making plans to scrape and repaint those rusty old pearly gates.

Traveling with Friends

One of the themes of this book is what friendships have meant to Marian and me. On a number of vacations, we have been joined by friends who made these trips much more pleasant and interesting. Donn Vickers and Sharon Sachs are high-energy, delightful traveling companions always eager to search for something interesting to do or see.

"Are you sitting down? How would you like to add a wedding to our trip to England?" asked Donn. He knew a pastor in Moffat, Scotland, and had planned his wedding there.

Arriving in Moffat, we had a nice lunch with the minister and proceeded to the large Presbyterian church. After the ceremony, we went shopping for woolens, and after dinner went to a fiddle festival at the local high school, which turned into a reception for the newlyweds.

Several years later, the four of us decided to go to Nova Scotia to test whether a big thirty-two-foot RV would be a good investment after Marian and I retired. (It wouldn't. The vehicle was hard to park and level.) We opted to stay at B and Bs at night so we could have a comfortable bed, privacy, and a decent shower.

Nova Scotia is like Ohio with water, but we especially enjoyed the scenic, hilly northern coast where our B-and-B breakfast featured sweet, native blueberries: pancakes, scones, jelly, and syrup. The trip even included an annual buskers (minstrel) convention in Halifax.

Several years later, we arranged a trip to Tuscany. We took turns shopping and making dinner. We usually went to a restaurant for one meal a day, often at a restaurant high on a mountain across the valley. Adjacent hills were in bloom with swaths of light-blue irises providing a handsome setting.

The house we rented sat in the middle of Sangiovese vineyards where Chianti is made. I visited one winemaker at the foot of our lane. "How long has your family been making wine here?"

His answer was startling. "Two thousand years."

Travel is so enlightening.

Tom and Rose Fawcett

As a couple, Tom and Rose were not known for luxury living. Tom was the chief financial officer at the Ross Division of Abbott Laboratories. He and I did not have much day-to-day exchange, but we were in meetings together at least weekly. One day I mentioned that my wife and I were planning to go back to the inside passage in Alaska, where we had once been on a small boat cruise.

He said he would like to do that too, so I said let's do it together.

A week before the trip, Tom had a very serious heart attack. Marian and I went to Alaska alone. When we returned, Tom was still in the hospital. I visited and told him we would go again *if* he would get well. He recovered, and we made reservations for the following summer. We decided to go first class.

Tom and Rose were good traveling companions. Rose had never been on a cruise and was delighted with every treat. Tom had a secret: he had told his wife that he had stopped smoking, but he lied. After each meal, he disappeared for fifteen minutes. He would sneak outside to the afterdeck, smoke, eat a few mints, and return. I don't think Rose ever caught on.

When we landed in Vancouver after the cruise, we took the Rocky Mountaineer train across Canada, stopping at Kamloops and Banff. The train terminated in Calgary, where we caught the plane to Columbus. We had spent two weeks together, and we enjoyed every minute of it.

Steve and Barbara Borik

One evening at a standup Christmas cocktail party, Barbara Borik, wife of our human resources vice president, Steve, remarked that she would love to go to England, but they had never applied for passports. Steve was not eager to undertake the trip but wanted to please his wife. I piped up and said that we would be pleased to show them around. We decided that night to do it, and we planned a two-week self-guided tour.

We began in London, renting a suite at 11 Cadogan Gardens, one of those high-end boutique hotels, for $700 per night. (Divided by four people, we did not consider the price outrageous.) The hotel was located in a row of nineteenth-century brick townhomes near an Underground stop. We had our own house with the key to the front door. Each morning we would call in a breakfast order, and a tuxedoed waiter would come up the back stairs and set a beautiful table in the living room of the suite, which overlooked a small park.

Steve was a very big man in both height and weight, sardonic, moody, and brilliant. He was impressed with Cadogan Gardens.

After several days of sightseeing in London, we set off for Stonehenge, Bath, the Lake Country, Inverness above Loch Ness, and back to London, stopping along the way to visit castles and other typical tourist attractions.

We drove a van, and Steve said he would try driving after the stop in the Lake Country. During a walk around the beautiful lake at Buttermere, Steve twisted his ankle badly. I always claimed he did it purposely so he wouldn't have to drive on the left side of the road.

We enjoyed the trip so much that we decided to tour Italy the next year, but taking public transportation instead of driving. We landed in Milan and soon learned that Steve's large size was a serious liability in showers, in bus seats, and elsewhere. He was grumpy about his discomfort.

The highlight of the trip was Venice. We celebrated Barb's birthday one evening with a ride in a gondola on a night with a full moon. During the boat ride, Barb started to cry and said, "I am so happy."

The day we were to go to Pompeii, Steve stormed off the bus because his knees wouldn't fit in the bus seat. However, that day he and Barb traveled by public transportation to Herculaneum and had a good experience.

We never traveled overseas together again, but we remained good friends for many years, visiting them in Pensacola, Florida, after Steve retired.

Whit Tussing and his mother, M.L. (Mary Lou)

Sometime in the nineties, my back and legs started to ache, and I walked with a cane. I had an idea: Why not ask Whit Tussing, the young architect who had helped us design the farmhouse and bank, if he would like to drive us around England? He said yes immediately. His mom was a good friend, and I asked her if she would like to come along, at her expense.

When we arrived in England, we went to the car rental desk, where we were offered an automatic transmission upgrade in a commodious Kia van. I was suspicious about a Korean-made car that was new in the market, but it was wonderful, except for a garish, bright-red-and-blue interior.

Our first stop was in a remote village near Stonehenge where the local pub featured Sticky Toffee Pudding for dessert—a delicious diabetic's horror. Whit was so impressed he learned to make it in Ohio when we returned.

Like typical tourists, we enjoyed it all. Memories piled on good memories. The Scottish highlands were more dramatic than I had remembered, but the Loch Ness monster was nowhere to be seen. In Inverness the restaurant we had selected was full, so we went to another one nearby and had an extraordinary steak dinner featuring delicious Scotch beef. Travel is best when unexpected things happen that remain in your notebook of fond memories.

Our last few days were in London, including several evenings at the theater. We lodged at one of those converted row houses that line London streets, at a quarter the cost of a downtown hotel. Whit especially enjoyed a visit to the Soane Museum in Lincoln Fields. Soane was one of the most famous English architects and a compulsive collector of architectural remnants. The house is a treasure of architectural artifacts and features, such as a picture gallery that folds back to reveal a three-story atrium.

Travel with good friends enhances and intensifies personal relationships, revealing our quirky selves not possible in polite circumstances at home.

Keith Boyle

Keith was a painting professor at Stanford University who lived across the street from us in Palo Alto. He loved Matisse, his favorite artist. He and I traveled to Washington, DC, to view a massive retrospective at the National Gallery. We took rooms at the renovated Willard Hotel, where U. S. Grant once spent afternoons smoking and having a whiskey. The Matisse show was very large, so we returned over two days to enjoy it.

On the third day, we took Amtrak to Philadelphia to see the Barnes collection in Merion, Pennsylvania. Dr. Barnes had known Matisse and commissioned a huge mural for his home. He also bought many other famous Matisse paintings (e.g., "The Music Lesson") housed in the Barnes collection. When we entered the main hall where the large mural was installed, I noticed that Keith started to cry.

Had a great time, wish you were there.

About Writing

When was the last time you handwrote a long letter? Letter writing was once a high art. No longer. Folks tweet, dash off e-mails, and send a few postcards from a vacation site. During World War II, I wrote a letter every day to Uncle Dick, who was stationed in India. Letter writing was my introduction to the written form.

In high school, I wrote a weekly gossip column for the school newspaper. The items were very tame, and the juicy stories never saw print. We knew that two classmates were sleeping together, and the boy always carried some pornography with him that he shared in gym class. Lou Broza had a bottle of whiskey in his locker and would nip from it between classes. That wonderful gossip never made it into my column, but the column was well read nevertheless. Students wanted to see if their names had been mentioned. I also worked on the yearbook and was assigned to write those short statements characterizing each student.

When I started to work as a salesman, I wrote a brief report on every sales call. My management told me they enjoyed my reports because I laced them with anecdotes and humor. After discharge from the army, I was asked to return to the home office to help with sales training and to develop sales presentations. I wrote hundreds of long and short documents. We produced four new sales presentations a year, usually based on a scientific article that discussed an aspect of infant nutrition. Everything I drafted was read aloud by the sales manager, Dave Cox, who made suggestions and demanded changes when needed. I became a more careful writer, writing straightforward, unembellished prose.

The company sent me to the Rensselaer Polytechnic Institute for a weeklong course in technical writing. I absorbed many of their caveats, such as never begin a sentence with "there are" or "it is." After returning from that instruction, I was even more aware of the need for clarity and simple construction.

When Marian and I moved to the Saratoga Retirement Community in 2006, I joined a writers group. Active members met monthly to read something they had written. Their material was varied, ranging from memories of trips abroad to fanciful stories based on biblical characters. I began to write short biographical vignettes that I named "VIN YETS." After two years, I self-published my first book.

As the years went by, I valued the writing process more. The messy first draft sounded like a dictated recording, followed by the process of editing, reediting, and reediting until most of the fluff had disappeared.

My spelling was never exemplary. The Apple computer dictionary corrected my lousy spelling. Google searches helped me recall places where I had traveled, and James Thurber's spirit hovered over me to add a bit of humor whenever I could. The nicest compliment I ever had about my writing came from a niece who said, "When I read your VIN YETS, I can hear you talking."

I have a secret fantasy about my books. Fifty years from now, some graduate student at Princeton will discover my books and declare that she had found a definitive source about life and culture from 1930 to early in the 2000s.

Fat chance.

REMEMBRANCE OF THINGS PAST

(with apologies to Marcel Proust)

Our brains are astounding. An experience is transformed into tiny bits of protein that are stored for a lifetime. These bits persist and pop out unexpectedly and set off a chain of other protein bits related to them.

Rides in the New Car

Dad was late coming home for dinner one evening in the summer of 1937. A shiny, new black Chevrolet sedan pulled up at the curb—the family's first car. Dad was very proud, and after dinner we went for a ride. So began an entertainment that lasted decades: taking rides into the countryside with no particular destination, just the ride as entertainment.

Over time we accumulated destinations and stops along the way. One was a ride to a favorite fruit stand in the countryside near West Chester. We bought fruit in season, watermelons and sweet corn in summer, cider in the fall, and half bushels of apples. The stand also sold homemade ice cream. The most delicious was the rich purple-black raspberry ice cream served in a cup cone. Like the fruit, that ice cream was seasonal, available for only a summer month.

The town of Swarthmore lay in a different direction. A ten-acre lake was located near the college. We would rent a rowboat for an hour and row slowly around the lake. It was there that I first learned to row a boat, though rowing a boat while facing the stern always seemed peculiar to me. It made much more sense to face in the direction you rowed, but physics and tradition topped reason.

After we bought a car, we often traveled to Lancaster to visit my parents' parents. This too became an excuse for treats. Halfway from Philadelphia to Lancaster, a small cow town, Exton, had a dairy where homemade caramels were offered for sale. The most unusual was a toffee-flavored one with black walnuts my parents considered a delicacy. I preferred the plain caramel.

Nearer Lancaster lay Coatesville, a nondescript town with the Lukens steel mill and a YMCA that served Sunday dinners in a cafeteria. The family would troop up to the second-floor restaurant and select homemade chicken and dumplings, mashed potatoes with gravy, and sweet corn, with apple pie for dessert. Many years later, the Pennsylvania turnpike bypassed Coatesville, the steel mill closed, and it is unlikely that the chicken dinners are served anymore.

Ours was a family of five, so Mother and Dad sat in the front seat of the car. All three brothers fought to be the one selected to sit between my parents. Because I was the youngest and smallest, I normally was chosen to sit in the middle. However, if the twins became too rowdy in the back seat, I would be displaced by the perpetrator.

The car had no heater, so in the winter everyone but the driver spread a heavy blanket over their lap and legs. The car was not only a mode of transportation but also our primary form of entertainment in those days.

TV, Pac Man, and computers were far in the future.

The Bank:
Second Thoughts

It took seven years to complete the restoration of the Glenford Bank. We lived in it for seven years. Adding the cost of renovation of the old barn nearby and the extra property purchased, we spent nearly three quarters of a million dollars on the project. We bought the bank for $19,000. We sold it at auction for $183,000. You do the math. I think we know the definition of a white elephant. Would I do it again? In a minute.

What cost so much? The building was a shell. We needed a well, a sewer system, a new roof, new sump pumps with a new drainage system, a kitchen, and two new bathrooms, including a Jacuzzi tub. The woodwork needed restoration. New oak moldings needed to be recreated. (New molding cutters were seventy-five dollars each, and we required twelve new ones.) We found an old candlestick phone for the telephone booth in the rotunda, but the booth needed to be rewired. Oh, and we needed a new electrical panel, a new boiler, an air-conditioning system, and concrete drilling to make the two fireplaces into gas fireplaces. The oak wood floors needed sanding and refinishing. Every pane of glass had to be replaced and caulked. New downspouts had to be fashioned. New outside doors had to be designed, built, and installed.

We bought new furniture to maintain the Arts and Crafts décor. We traveled to antique shows to find art pottery of the period, books by Elbert Hubbard of the Roycroft community, original Stickley chairs and side tables, Arts and Crafts candlesticks, and appropriate andirons for the fireplaces. When we were threatened by development across the street, we helped buy the property and had it transformed into a park—landscaped, of course. The direction pointer on the roof was full of bullet holes, so we had it sent to Indiana to be reconstructed in copper.

Did I ever think about all the money we were spending? Yes, but the project felt like an assignment to save and restore a wonderful old building. I hired an historian, Kathy Mast Kane, to write the bank's history, and we paid her to put the place on the National Register of Historic Places. Nothing was too good for the project.

Did we fret about procedure? Not enough. A professional restorer would have fixed the roof first, which required a change in the roof design because the original contractors ran out of money and installed a leaky flat roof instead of a sloped one. We were too concerned with minutiae. We even had an analysis of the exterior grout made so when Jim Sturgeon tuck-pointed a few places, it would match. It didn't, probably because he didn't use creek bed sand from Jonathan Creek like the original bricklayers did. When architect Whit Tussing recommended some lights on the exterior of building, I said no. We installed six 1920-style streetlights at the curb, with electric eyes so they would automatically light at dusk.

Happiness is lavishing care on a beautiful old building, one that was one of a kind, out of context in an old farm village, and filled with ghosts of the interesting folks who built it and worked there. Ever since 1932, when the bank was abandoned, the kids in the town played there. They played badminton, basketball, and crawled into the attic, probably to smoke and tell off-color jokes.

Amen and amen.

'Til Death Us Do Part

Living in assisted living, we lose a resident at least once a month. Anne Zane died very suddenly. She came to dinner one evening, and she was gone by morning. She had the loudest sneeze in the dining room, and we knew she would sneeze at least four times once she started. After the third sneeze, our tablemates would applaud.

Donal O'Regen faded more slowly. He progressed slowly from hearty to frail. I once called him "Donald," and he became incensed. "No, the name is Donal." He was very Irish with a beautiful Irish accent. He loved to sing, and when we moved into assisted living, he often sang loudly in the dining room, disrupting whatever peace we had. He had a sharp temper, and if something displeased him, he would bark his objection. Now he is gone.

Carolyn was a long time resident who died in 2012. She was ill tempered and once announced, "This place is nothing but a goddamn warehouse."

My wife Marian noted the other day, "Do you realize that this is the last place we will ever live?"

As a matter of fact, I recently thought I had lost Marian. About nine months ago, she began to be lethargic, sleeping in her chair all day long. She stopped doing daily chores and only picked at her food. The situation became so critical we made an appointment with our internist to diagnose what was going wrong. He ordered blood tests and discovered that her thyroid metabolism was seriously out of kilter. Marian had "apathetic hyperthyroidism," a frequent complication of the elderly causing extreme lethargy. He recommended that we see an endocrinologist, who agreed that her thyroid dose was too high, but it would take six weeks to see if a lower dose had any effect. It didn't. Then our internist restudied her meds and realized that she was still taking a powerful sleeping tablet he had prescribed years before. In addition to too much Synthroid, her blood pressure med was too high. Our daughter and son-in-law, both experienced nurses, determined that she was badly dehydrated.

We also remembered that about the time she started failing, we had arranged that the staff give her her prescriptions every day instead of letting her supervise her own medicines. It is likely she had not been taking full dosages then suddenly received every drug every day.

The situation was so serious that when I woke each morning, I would look to see if she were still alive.

After correcting the dosages and getting rehydrated, she began to respond quickly. An appetite stimulant worked well and she gained thirty pounds. Her life has returned, although with more memory loss.

We all face mortality. When I think about it, I conclude that it would be a bother and inconvenient at this time. Our age seems not to matter. Many of our residents are ninety or older and are healthy. Genetics may be the most important factor affecting longevity. Mother lived until she was almost ninety, and her brother is in his mid-nineties.

That might mean I have another ten years to fret about our national debt and too much government intervention.

WHAT HAVE YOU FORGOTTEN?

A resident walked down the hall while we were waiting for dinner and asked, "What year was the attack on Pearl Harbor? Was it 1944?"

Marian answered, "December 7, 1941."

"Do you remember where you were when you heard?"

"Yes, I was ironing and listening to the radio. They canceled regular programming."

Think of all you things you can't remember or haven't thought of in decades. Strange. Your brain is filled with chemicals, most gathered together in teeny, complicated proteins, each with a specific memory—millions of them. Some are lurking, some hiding in plain sight, and some are immediately available to a request for recall.

Recently I looked at an illustrated catalogue of the things we sold at auction when we moved to California. There among other familiar items was a colorful wall sculpture I felt I had never seen before. I asked my brain to go through the memory bank to help me identify the piece. It took a few moments; then memories flooded.

Of course: Queen Brooks; Columbus, Ohio; her house; hanging on the wall; reasonable price; recollections of her trip to Ghana: my carved cane; the bicycle she decorated; fried chicken luncheon with Donn and Queen; health insurance for starving artists . . . and a cascade of other thoughts. What a miracle. Tickle those little memory proteins, and they bloom.

Search! Did you live in a city where if you had chickenpox, whooping cough, or measles, the health department would stop by and put a yellow quarantine sticker on your front door?

Search! Do you remember fixing a flat inner tube with a patch kit or floating on an inner tube on the creek? Your first kiss? What you wore to the senior prom? Can you recall your childhood telephone number? Some thoughts are harder to retrieve than others.

Don't worry about it. We forget things every day. We elderly are supposedly luxuriating in golden memories. That's a bunch of baloney. Those golden memory proteins are slowly turning to mush.

FOOD JUNKIES

For several decades, we lived thirty miles east of Columbus. I'd leave the office after 5:30, pick up Marian at Mt. Carmel, and we would head home. But instead of cooking after we arrived home, we would stop along the way and eat some junk food, often eaten in the car while driving east. We knew every fast food joint along the way: Wendy's, McDonald's, Subway, Arby's, Dairy Queen, White Castle, and others. It was shameful, but what the hell. It was better than cooking and cleaning the kitchen at eight in the evening. Each fast food emporium offered a favorite.

Arby's sold a roast beef sandwich made from a fake beef roast shaved thin and piled high. It was not the beef we enjoyed, but the Arby sauce made from mayonnaise and horseradish. They called it "horsey sauce," and it was delicious.

Subway sells a foot-long meat sandwich on which you could select a choice of fresh veggies. We tended to eat the same sandwich nightly: ham and cheese with onions, green bell peppers, lettuce, and mayo. For many years we ordered foot-longs, but in time we realized that six inches would do just fine, particularly if we also ordered potato chips. Subway offered chicken salad from time to time, and we selected that. Occasionally we ordered a drippy meatball sandwich, but it was tough to eat and steer the car careening down the highway.

Ah McDonald's! The first franchise in Columbus in the 1950s was franchised by Herb Huffman, a musician who was the first choir director of the Columbus Boys Choir located in Princeton, New Jersey. Located in the east end, we marveled at the golden arches, the sign telling how many millions of hamburgers sold, and the cheeseburgers with french fries sold for a very reasonable price. Marian and I have eaten thousands of McDonald's products over the decades, and still do. Whenever we have an afternoon doctor's appointment in Palo Alto, we leave early and go to the McDonald's near the Route 85/de Anza exit. I order the number eight meal, a Southern-style battered chicken sandwich with fries and a drink. The chicken has two thinly sliced dill pickles that give the sandwich its luster. Marian orders a chocolate milkshake with whipped cream and a cherry. When we eat there at breakfast time, we covet a sausage McMuffin with egg, one of God's great masterpieces. It is true that McDonald's french fries are very good, until they get cold, and then they become as pasty and soggy as everyone else's.

Wendy's originated in Columbus when Dave Thomas opened a hamburger store in the heart of downtown, minutes from where Marian and I worked. The hamburger was square and tasty. They also sold chili and some salads. Our favorite was the taco salad: chili on a bed of lettuce topped with tortilla chips. But the Wendy's highlight was the chocolate milkshake called a Frosty. Conservatively, Marian sipped thousands of them in her lifetime.

White Castle was also headquartered in Columbus. Their hamburger became affectionately known as a "slider." It was very strange, but delicious. It was only a small three-inch square by a quarter inch thick flat, preformed ground beef with holes in it for rapid cooking. Several dozen burgers were placed on a hotplate, smothered with chopped onions, and steamed. A small bun was placed on top until the meat was cooked then scooped onto the lower half of the roll with a pickle slice and placed in a cardboard jacket. Normally I ordered six at a time with a diet cola. (You could ask for a squirt of ketchup.)

Our adoration of junk food extends to Jack in the Box, Dairy Queen, and others as necessity might require. Dairy Queen sells a tasty strawberry sundae with garish, bright-red strawberry gel and fruit that tastes just right. Jack in the Box sells a good milkshake that is so thick that it must melt for a few minutes before you can suck it up with a straw.

Being a fast-food junkie has not affected our longevity. It is probably the excess salt and fat that makes that food taste so good and adds to our years. Marian and I have often said we should write a book about junk food. We are experienced aficionados.

Fast junk food is much, much better than bean sprouts, artichokes, and avocados. Those are not sold at Carl Jr's.

IN JAIL

This is the second time that Marian and I have been in jail, quarantined, and been fed in our cells. A year ago, a nurse came into my bedroom and said, "We are sending you out. You fainted." They called 911, and in a few minutes I was in an ambulance bumping my way to the hospital. I was suffering from the flu, which, when diagnosed, was the dreaded norovirus, the enemy of all retirement communities. The flu can spread like lighted gasoline among the elderly. Retirement community management typically takes immediate measures to isolate sick folks.

Dehydration is the most severe symptom, the result of violent nausea and diarrhea. In my case, four or five bags of IV fluid were all I needed to recover sufficiently to be discharged from the hospital. When I returned to my apartment, I was informed that the building was closed down: no activities, no dining room. We were to stay in our rooms until the "all clear" was pronounced. The shutdown lasted four or five days. Thank God for computers and TV to keep us from going stir crazy.

Three weeks ago, a head cold seemed to worsen. Marian and I began to eat alone so I wouldn't pass the cold around, but the head cold lingered, with modest diarrhea and no nausea. I was improving. Then Marian went down—

really down. A virulent flu had struck. Three times we needed to call maintenance to deep clean the rugs. She was miserable, and very ill for twenty-four hours, and then the symptoms disappeared.

Management acted quickly and closed the place down again. Our meals were served in our rooms. The damage was done. Suddenly the bad bug decided I was susceptible, and down I went. Way down—way, way down. I started drinking Gatorade to make sure I was keeping electrolytes balanced, but the Gatorade would not stay down. Misery.

In twenty-four hours things began to abate, but I was feeling weak and woozy. I was scheduled to host an open house in the library, but they asked me not to go to the other buildings. I was in jail for the duration. And the duration went on and on for over a week. When we finally went to the dining room for lunch, it was like a reunion. "Did you get sick?" "Glad you were spared; it was terrible." It felt like a college reunion.

Our apartment dining room table was filled with uneaten food, sets of plastic tableware, napkins, and Styrofoam boxes. After we could keep down solid food, we always ordered the same breakfast: a piece of white toast and a strip of bacon. (In England they call this breakfast sandwich a *butty*.) It is perfect prisoner food.

Last October we had a flu shot. It didn't work.

A Brush with Karl Marx

In the late 1960s, I chaired a community coalition titled The Urban Education Coalition in Columbus. The organization focused on school reform and comprised fifty or so organizations with an interest in school performance. The groups were both conservative and liberal.

One of the member organizations was the South Side Settlement House, one of the largest in Columbus, funded by the Episcopalians. The director and I became friends. and he decided to take a yearlong sabbatical in England at the London School of Economics.

While he was studying in London, I took a business trip there. He and his wife invited me to lunch at their home in Highgate. The rented house was one of those unpretentious row houses with a small fenced front yard, alcove windows in the parlor, high ceilings, and a dull, musty smell. Lunch was a modest salad with a piece of cake for dessert. (Before lunch he served a highball and a dish of raisins mixed with blanched peanuts, a splendid combination that I had never eaten before.)

After lunch he said that he had an idea. "Let's walk to the Highgate Cemetery where a number of famous people are buried." The most famous resident is Karl Marx, but there are many other well-known internees. The cemetery is high Victorian with ersatz gothic gates, mausoleums, and tombstones. Statues abound. The trees and shrubs are mature, giving the feeling of an old, overgrown, shaded park.

We went directly to the Marx tomb, where a larger-than-life bronze head on a pedestal dominated the plot. My friend insisted on posing me by the sculpture for a photograph.

He then began to tease me that he planned to send a copy of the picture to the *Columbus Dispatch* so the city could see where my allegiances were. To be honest, I was fearful that the rascal would do that, but he didn't. My reputation remained intact.

Marx is dead, and communism has turned into a police state again, but I remain a grateful capitalist.

ALIENS

A UFO supposedly crashed in Roswell, New Mexico, in 1947, when the US Army retrieved the machine and captured the aliens inside. But it took until the late 1970s before the alien craze came to full fruition Suddenly UFOs and aliens became a cause célèbre, and popular culture had a new craze.

The movie *Close Encounters of the Third Kind* was followed by *E.T. the Extra-Terrestrial*. The History Channel produced documentaries pointing out how frequently earth had been visited by aliens and what evidence "proved" it. At Hewlett-Packard, R and D chief Barney Oliver developed and implemented Project Cyclops, looking for intelligent life in outer space. (Near the Palo Alto exit on Highway 280, you can still see the huge radio telescope set up for the program.) Dozens of people claimed they were in touch with aliens telepathically. Search Google for "contacting aliens," and there are 1,930,000 hits in 0.28 seconds. Engineers at the Stanford Research Institute went into deep trances, hoping to learn about energy uses by aliens. *Star Trek* became one of the most popular TV shows, and *Star Wars* was projected in movie theaters.

None of this seems to have turned up anything concrete that earth humans can believe. Our mistake may be that we expect to find aliens similar to ourselves. Most graphic representations portray humanoid creatures, sometimes with one eye and antennas extending from an enlarged brain. Nonsense. Intelligent life might simply be unformed protoplasm and already here.

Perhaps the opposite is the case—aliens have taken our human form and are walking among us. (Who is that person sitting by your side?)

What we know for sure is that space will always intrigue us. We will always wonder if we are the only intelligent life forms that exist. You can bet that somewhere today a psychologist is writing a paper entitled, "The Consequences of Discovering Life in Outer Space." There will be more movies and plays like Orson Welles' *War of the Worlds* broadcast in October 1938.

Because the cosmos is so unlimited, we will never be able to search it in our lifetime. Only if cogent aliens appear in reality will we ever be satisfied whether intelligent life exists out there. It's their move.

I wonder whether they enjoy vodka martinis.

EDUCATIONAL REFORM: RADICAL SECOND THOUGHTS

For six years of my adult life, I was paid to think about school reform, first as a fellow in the National Program for Educational Leadership and then in the Palo Alto School District in a planning exercise we labeled Project Redesign. The word *paradigm* was one of our overused buzzwords. We never changed the Palo Alto paradigm (a classroom-centered school system) even though a former board member, Barney Oliver, was head of research and development at Hewlett-Packard. Our final report never mentioned computers.

The United States spends billions annually (about 5 percent of GDP) on schooling. College has nearly priced itself out of business.

The primary reason schooling is so expensive is the existing paradigm of utilizing teachers or professors to teach students. Students en masse sit to be instructed by a teacher, perhaps thirty students in a classroom or hundreds in a college lecture hall. Society has agreed that teachers and professors should be paid a living wage.

What if you were required to reduce the cost of education by two-thirds or more and simultaneously improve education output? Impossible? No, but the paradigm must be changed radically if cost reduction and educational improvement are to be achieved.

Most school buildings and teachers would be eliminated. Some old buildings or new ones would be designed with extensive computer labs where students would follow an e-learning curriculum at their pace. That would be a macro-change, but a micro-change is also required. For one hour a day, every student would be required to concentrate on communication skills: writing, reading, speaking, and listening. Emphasis should be on writing letters to friends, short stories, essays on public issues, etc. Adult advancement is often related to the ability to conceive fresh ideas and convey those ideas with the written or spoken word.

Schools now operate on the principle of in loco parentis, i.e. in place of a parent.

Most of us have been blessed with a close attachment to a beloved teacher, but as important as they are, they are not a substitute for a loving and supportive family.

In the time spent in the Third World, I have learned that mothers usually love and care for their children to the best of their ability, no matter how poor they are. Schools will never be able to substitute for loving parents. Education needs to do no harm to a student's psyche. Its task is to guide the learning process. Most teachers will become superfluous. Parents never will.

The global Internet has eliminated the need to spoon-feed children in small bits in classrooms dominated by a teacher. However, brilliant minds must think through how to attach students to that incredible computer world in humane and efficient ways.

Perhaps you already know about the Khan Academy, whose motto is, "Learn Almost Anything for Free." Ten million students, old and young, are taking these courses. Our world has become one world, with knowledge readily available to all. In the short term, things may not change. In the long run, they will. Classrooms, degrees, and Harvard will cease to exist.

No more pencils, no more books, no more teachers' dirty looks.

I'm Really Pissed

Sometimes anger burns. I mean really burns. Why can't people understand how they are being mislead, taken advantage of, used, duped, scammed, or lied to? Most people are too trusting, too naïve, and too accepting. I am not immune.

The evening news showed a group of protesters screaming about the evils of business, as if all businessmen were ruthless, fat, cigar smokers. Some probably are, but most are not. Where do those protesters think jobs come from? The nation struggles with job creation, but the protestors bite the hand that feeds them. I wonder where protestors get money for their cell phones, printed posters, tents, food, and transportation to the protest. Probably from their salaries or a misguided donor.

Once upon a time, I was charged with vetting our advertising and assuring management that what we said in our promotion was factually correct and not meant to mislead. Yes, I was assigned to keep us honest. My title at that time was director of Business Practices. I was the house ethicist, and I tried to be rigorous. I become very irritated when all businessmen are condemned.

It's frustrating too when I hear groups like the Center for Science in the Public Interest complain that a pharmaceutical company was involved in a piece of published science. During and after World War II, our government began giving large grants to universities for pharmaceutical research. But who makes and markets prescription drugs? Not the government, but Pfizer, Eli Lily, Abbott, and dozens of others. They too provide grants to independent investigators in new drug development. The pharmaceutical industry is an equal partner of the academic/government coalition. Most medical journals are juried to verify and analyze submitted papers. The FDA decides which drugs may be marketed and which claims may be made. Some previous estimates suggest that a new drug takes five years and five billion dollars to succeed. Are there sometimes greed and excessive profits in the drug system? Sometimes, but would you prefer to eliminate antibiotics, painkillers, and insulin? I doubt it.

What really makes me mad are taxes of all kinds: sales taxes, income taxes, capital gains taxes, gas taxes, and all the dozens of others. What infuriates me is that I no longer know who imposed them, who profits from them, what the money is used for, or why government asks for more when we already have a massive debt. I do not approve of the billions spent in Afghanistan, but I am powerless to do anything about it. I e-mail my representatives and senators and get back dismissive boilerplate letters written by staff members. My tax anger stems from my powerlessness to impact the system.

Now that I am in my golden years, I am very upset by my declining body and memory. I should exercise more, but when I walk more than a hundred feet, my right knee starts to ache. The array of drugs I take is embarrassing, but they keep me going, and my company insurance pays for $2,500 of them each year. Sometimes I have difficulty remembering specific words; I can visualize a microwave, but the other day I couldn't think of the word. Last names disappear like a bag of potato chips—rapidly. I become upset when I hear someone complaining about something they could avoid easily, like too many sweetened foods on the menu. For God's sake, eat fruit!

Worst of all are the folks who are ideologues, people who are sure that they are correct about everything. Everything is black or white, no shades of gray permitted. It's okay to hold strong opinions, but as a nephew says, "I am absolutely sure, but I could be wrong." This applies to religion, politics, sports, and everything else. You and I could be wrong, misinformed, incorrectly taught, or misled. It was a great day when I discovered that though something was in writing, it could still be wrong.

In recent years, I have become more intolerant, quicker to anger, and more skeptical. Whoopee, I am now officially a grumpy old man.

A Glut of Advertising

Several Sundays ago, I counted the number of television commercials during *CBS Sunday Morning*. I counted fifty. They left me in a blur. One ran into the next oftem with no pause, and I became confused where one started and where one ended. For a while, British telly commercials faded to black so you knew where one ended and the next started. I am particularly confused by the commercials that pretend to set up a real-life drama and then conclude with a corporate logo. I am also confused by the jumpy, quick-cut, slice-of-life shots that are irrelevant to the product presentation.

A saying among marketing people is, "I am wasting half my money, but I don't know which half."

For the first half of my business career, I managed sales promotion and advertising for a company that increased from twelve million in annual sales to a billion dollars in sales. I had a masterful sales mentor, Dave Cox, whose natural sense of promotion bordered on genius. He taught me the basic principles of good advertising, and we rarely strayed from them.

1. Lodge the name of the product.
2. Describe what the product is for.

3. Present the most relevant product preference features.

4. Make sure the customer will see an ad at least six times.

5. Always include necessary caveats.

6. Coordinate direct mail, magazine advertising, and salesman presentations to a common theme.

7. Discount your effectiveness by your competitors' dollar expenditures.

After fulfilling those principles, I was encouraged to be as creative as I wanted, assuming that cleverness is relevant. We sold infant formula. I once ran an ad that began, "Similac Is Second Best." (Breast-feeding is the best way to feed a baby.)

Our success was more than a two-man show. Our New York agency was William Douglas McAdams, whose president was Arthur (Artie) Sackler. In addition to his ability to make money, Artie was a world-renowned philanthropist with a special emphasis on monumental Chinese art. He would collect the finest items available throughout the world and store them in warehouses all over New York. His Chinese collection is now seen in the Sackler Gallery on the Smithsonian mall in Washington, DC. For a while, he had a private office at the Metropolitan Art Museum in New York where his terracotta collection was stored. The Temple of Dendur was installed in the Sackler Wing at the Met in 1978.

His marketing skill resided in his ability to invent new media outlets and persuade his clients to advertise in them. For example, he invented *Medical Tribune,* a daily tabloid newspaper for doctors. For years we bought two half pages every day, billed at 17.65 percent to the agency. Think big, spend big. Only the best would do: food, wine, theater, design, art, etc. He even tried to get us to fund Masterpiece Theater with Alistair Cooke. He was scary but brilliant. Humility and modesty were not his virtues. At agency meetings, his ideas flowed like Niagara Falls.

But my best work was in the creation of sales promotion materials. I had a trick that worked for me for years: I would imagine I was sitting in a doctor's office talking to him or her about our latest campaign. But marketing success has its own restraints. Either the product is better than what's available or it is not. In the 1950s, most GPs and pediatricians fed babies evaporated milk with Dextri Maltose. Breast-feeding was out of favor, and in a decade, we were feeding half the infants in the United States.

Here's a test to evaluate a good TV ad. If after ten seconds you don't know what product an ad is selling, the client is wasting his or her money.

Wonderful advertising is not mysterious, nor often creative.

"Just the facts, mam."

Shiva Defines the Universe

As early as the seventh century and refined by the tenth, the pantheon of Hindu gods included the Shiva Nataraja, better known as the dancing Shiva. It is astounding that those Indian sages understood so much about the nature of the universe, human qualities, and political philosophy. I had seen small bronzes of the dancing Shiva before but thought it weird that someone would have four arms. I did not understand that they represented varied manifestations of the god.

When we lived in Palo Alto, I was befriended by Dr. Mark Markley, who was working at the Stanford Reasearch Institute. He was a designated futurist who searched the past for elements of advanced wisdom. Among those he wrote about were the ancient Christian mystics whose visions and insights influenced religious practices and the Hindu sages who described the pantheon of Hindu gods.

The dancing Shiva is an astounding portrayal of cosmic energy, shimmering as does the atom and the cosmos. In 2004, the Indian government presented a two-meter (six-foot) bronze statue of the nataraja to the European Organization for Nuclear Research (CERN) in Geneva with this statement: "The metaphor of the cosmic dance thus unifies ancient mythology, religious art, and modern physics."

The basic premise of the nataraja is simultaneous creation and destruction. One hand holds a flame, representing destruction, while another hand holds a small drum representing the beating of creation and time. The halo surrounding it all is the universe surrounded in flames.

Shiva is dancing frenetically, but his face is stoic and still. Another hand shows the palm out, signifying, "be without fear." The fourth arm and hand point to the dancing leg, the leg of freedom. The whole figure stands on a small dwarf or imp, the personification of evil, ignorance, or illusion. The bottom is a lotus leaf from which the Hindu god emerges.

It would take four or five pages to describe all of the exotic imagery and wisdom portrayed by the bronze. It is all very subtle. For example, Shiva wears an earring in both ears, one representing the male, and the other ear the female— the blend in all humans. Thousands of explanations of the bronze statues can be found on Google.

Shiva Nataraja came into my life in the seventies when the famous mythologist Joseph Campbell visited Palo Alto and explained it to us. His final words were, "All this is surrounded by silence." What an important thing to know in this hectic world. No matter how much noise we encounter, we are surrounded by silence.

Shall we dance?

THE HOUSE IN THE WOODS

Since we were married in 1955, Marian and I have lived in nine locations; three were apartments, and all the other locations were houses. In 1961, we bought a one-hundred-year-old farmhouse. After a three-year stint in Palo Alto in the early seventies, we returned to the farm again, and I itched to design and build a house where we could live all year. This was possible because of the profit we made from the sale of the house in Palo Alto. We had enough money to build and pay outright for a new home.

A prominent architect in Columbus told me that designing your home without an architect was like attempting brain surgery with no training. No matter, I forged ahead.

The house was to be high enough on the hill to see the pond. It would be two stories with a guest suite in the lower level and our quarters on the second floor. The house was a box, forty by forty feet. The roof was sloped so that the living room ceilings would be sixteen feet, the back wall of the living room twelve feet, and the back wall of our bedroom eight feet. The slope of the hill made it possible to walk out the back of the house into the garden. Local contractors did the construction.

My design flaws soon became apparent. I forgot to locate a proper front door (guests entered up the side steps), and we really needed a garage for the harsh Ohio winters. I swallowed my pride and hired an architect to correct my mistakes. Whitney, our architect, added a wing with an impressive entryway, a new sitting room, a garage, and a large basement storage space. Our revised home was a treat to come home to every day.

Living in the woods was the real treat. Every change of season provided a renewing experience. We added three quarters of an acre of professional landscaping, mostly in the rear of the house. Twenty-foot dogwoods near the pond bloomed in the spring when wildflowers blanketed the woods. Pileated woodpeckers screamed all year, and occasionally a white-tailed deer would pass our bedroom window. Mother raccoon discovered the cat food we kept outside on the deck, and she introduced her babies to the cache. A friend put out bluebird boxes, and bluebirds fledged three broods a year. Another friend put out beehives, and the berry bushes thrived.

When we left the farm to move into the bank building in the village nearby, the farm was bought by the literary director of the Thurber House, who continued to improve the house and property, using the old farmhouse to write books and poetry. He loves the woods and nature as much as we did, especially the morel mushrooms that appear on warm, moist May days.

A home and property like this one required work that never stopped: grass and paths to mow, flowers to deadhead, weeds to pull until frost brought a respite, firewood to stack, and koi to feed.

We loved every minute of it.

Truth and Errata

Memoirs have a certain danger about them. Are they accurate? Are they embellished? Do they represent the facts of what actually happened?

After publishing three books of "VIN YETs," I keep one copy of each book with a bright orange label on it. They are the books into which I pencil in corrections. As I read and reread what I have written, I record any mistakes, errors, typos, and false statements, just in case anyone would ever care to check to make me an honest man. Memoirs have the smell of self-indulgence about them, and mine are no exception. If there are any untruths in the books, it is because my memory has failed.

The nature of my errors are modest and relatively unimportant. Here are a few examples: Our condo in Sanibel was 1,800 square feet, not 2,800 square feet. That error has a history. We once took a tour of a condo on Captiva, the island north of Sanibel. The real estate agent gave you a silver dollar if you listened to her sales pitch. I told her that we were staying at the Lighthouse Resort and Club on Sanibel, where our condo was 3,200 square feet, and that her condos were just too small. She never corrected me, but she must have known that I was wrong. When I reread the piece entitled "Marian Goes

Shelling on Sanibel," I looked up the floor plan, and lo and behold—1,800 square feet. Whoops.

In my first book, we list the names of drugs that my daughter and I take daily. The names are no longer correct. Lipitor, Hytrin, and others have gone off patent, and we now take generic forms. Janice's drugs have expanded as her MS has progressed, so her list is incomplete. These errors are not my fault. Time has passed us by, and things have changed. The clock is ticking. Another VIN YET says we still own two weeks at our time share condo in Sanibel. Alas, we have sold those two weeks, and the book stands uncorrected. Time passage has robbed me of accuracy once again.

In another place, I say that I bought a Mac PC. No such computer exists. I should have written that I bought an Apple desktop, or simply an iMac. Well, don't shoot me.

The punctuation is somewhat different in each book because the publisher's line editor was different for each book. The first editor did not mind my habit of inserting ellipses (. . .) to extend a thought. The third editor hated them and changed the dots to semicolons. The second editor inserted dashes instead. Who cares?

There are some errors of grammar. Some plurals should be singular. Some past tenses should be present tenses. Too many commas flood the pages. These lapses should have been recognized by the editor. Apparently each editor didn't read the previous book so that the styles would match. Somehow I don't care. It exhausts me to think of the work to make it all consistent.

Most importantly, are the VIN YETs a fair and honest representation of what happened in real life? Have I exaggerated, or is it all authentic and as it really happened? (Autobiographers have been known to make things up.) My best answer: my memory is mostly visual, and I wrote as I "saw" things. Ergo, my memoirs are depictions of what I "see" in my memory, and that's the best I can do.

Take it or leave it!

What Is a
Continental Breakfast?

Hotels advertise that the continental breakfast is free. It's not. It's included in the price you paid for your room. The English are the most honest about it, "Bed and breakfast included." Most American motel chains now provide a "free" breakfast, but it wasn't always so. In my era, you paid seven dollars for off-flavored orange juice, two scrambled eggs with bacon (or link sausages), toast, and a cup of lousy coffee. It was not continental.

My former company has a manufacturing facility in Zwolle, Holland. When traveling there, one stays at a small hotel near the train station. Their continental breakfast was a surprise. When you sat down, a waitress brought a plate of cold sliced ham, some delicious sliced cheese garnished with fresh fruit, hearty untoasted bread and butter, and coffee or tea. Then something strange happened. The man at a nearby table had ordered a supplement. The odor was offensive—smoked kippered herring. The Dutch love smoked things, notably eel, but the stench spoiled my simple continental breakfast.

Every nation has some favored breakfast food. When breakfast was served at a hotel in Guatemala, the plate contained a fist-sized serving of refried beans with the eggs. Refried beans are a staple. Black beans are boiled the day before with garlic, onion, and cumin. After many hours of slow cooking, they are mashed and set aside to rest. The next morning they are reheated. They didn't seem refried to me.

A morning buffet in Bad Nauheim, Germany is elaborate and bountiful: meats, potatoes, fruit, cereal, yogurt, sweet pastries, juices, many forms of bread, and of course coffee. After that continental breakfast, you can skip lunch.

A full English breakfast is served in courses. First come the cereals and juice. Many cereals offered originated in America: Rice Krispies, cornflakes, or shredded wheat. But the British have their local favorites, Wheetabix and slow cooked oatmeal. The juices are often bottled or canned. The first course is followed by the hot course: eggs cooked to order, a rasher of ham or bacon, cold toast, and butter and jams, with a pot of coffee or strong tea.

But I am teasing you. Only one continental breakfast qualifies as the real thing, simple, elegant, and beyond delicious, in Paris. The essential ingredients are: freshly squeezed orange juice, thick with pulp and sweet as sin; and an honest buttery croissant fresh from the morning bakery, slightly crispy on the outside and soft as a marshmallow on the inside, served with creamery butter and homemade jams. Only one large croissant is served— no gluttony here. And that coffee. Dark and full-bodied with chocolate overtones; how do they do it?

I'm speechless!

I Scream, You Scream, We All Scream for Ice Cream

Many thousands of years ago, an Arab in northern Saudi Arabia poured some wine on mountain snow and invented the first sno-cone. When Marco Polo returned to Venice from China, he described the sherbet he had enjoyed. Slowly, iced cream made its way from Italy through Europe to England and then to America. Martha Washington and Dolly Madison served it to their guests, but it was not their invention. Both the French and the Brits refined the recipes with milk, eggs, flavors, and textures. Those gelatos in Italy with intense flavors and refreshing melting qualities always pleased. Ice cream speaks a universal language.

Over a lifetime, making homemade ice cream was a special treat. Our first churn was hand cranked, and the second was electrified. Someone discovered that if you salted ice, the temperature dropped enough to freeze custard in a rotating tank. Making ice cream was a celebration.

The Gordons lived across the small valley from our farm. Once a summer, they made a batch of hand-churned vanilla ice cream and invited friends in to share. Their large farm kitchen table displayed bowls of chocolate syrup, crushed strawberries, caramel, chopped peaches, nuts, and sprinkles. Virgil Gordon would scoop out bowls of ice cream for guests, and we would apply our favorite toppings.

As a child, Dad would walk to the drugstore and buy a quart of hand-packed Breyer's ice cream for dessert. The flavors varied, but it was usually vanilla, chocolate, or strawberry. I liked butter pecan, but the family didn't, so my favorite flavor was rare. Occasionally he would buy a brick of Neopolitan sliced so that each person got three flavors in every slab.

After dinner we often took a ride to buy an ice cream cone somewhere. The choice of a cone was serious business. The usual was a cake cone, but some shops offered cup cones. For a few pennies more, we could select a sugar cone that was darker, crispier, and more delicious. Fancy stores made waffle cones in back of the counter.

Each scoop of ice cream was a dime, and Dad would let us have two scoops, always different flavors sequenced so that you finished with your favorite flavor on the bottom. On rare occasions, we could have three scoops, but that led to melting by the time you got to the third scoop, and the dripping made for messy hands.

Childhood memories offer a collection of happy memories: chocolate and vanilla Dixie Cups eaten with a flat wooden spoon with a collectable photo under the lid, the lemon ice sold at dusk by a young man on a tricycle, the Good Humor truck with bells ringing as it approached the neighborhood. On hot summer afternoons, the sno-cone man walked by with his cart and a huge block of ice. For a few pennies, he shaved off a cup of ice, put it in a paper cone, and squirted a dash of sweetened syrup on it from colorful bottles of grape, orange, lime, cherry, root beer, vanilla, and chocolate flavors.

As adults we frequently filled our Honda Odyssey with neighbors and headed to Tom's Ice Cream Bowl in Zanesville for a tin roof. Tom's opened in 1948, and its décor has never been touched. Featuring homemade ice cream, they serve a tin roof sundae in large soup bowls, overflowing with a pint or more of vanilla ice cream smothered with chocolate syrup and a torrent of salty, greasy Spanish peanuts. The store was always crowded with customers waiting for a table.

Sometime in the eighties, I discovered a recipe for ice cream that I could make in five minutes. First, freeze about two cups of strawberries, peaches, or blueberries in season. Place the frozen fruit in a food processor with a cup of plain yogurt, sugar to taste, and a squeeze of lemon juice. Pulsing the mixture takes only a minute, and the result is delicious ice cream almost instantly. Dinner guests loved it, and so did I.

Even today, no meal seems complete without the hope of some rocky road, or pistachio, or butter pecan. Every once in a while, the waiter brings *two* scoops of butter pecan. Don't eat it too fast. Do you remember those ice cream headaches?

If heaven exists, it will have a Baskin-Robbins shop on every corner.

THE FOUR SEASONS
An Experiment in Stream of Consciousness

Winter

Midwinter in Saratoga, California. The temperature is fifty degrees, the sky is blue, flowers bloom, but it feels chilly.

As a child in Philadelphia, milk was delivered at dawn to the front door. The cream froze, and the cap on the bottle was nearly an inch above the lip. Mother would scoop off the frozen cream and let the milk thaw so she could make cocoa and toast for breakfast.

In Sanibel, Florida, in January, we sometimes experienced seventy degrees, but often had rain and blustery winds. In Ohio we once had a frightening ice storm on April 10.

In a science class at Cubberley High School in Palo Alto, the pupils noticed a rare snowfall. They raced to the windows to watch. Some of them had never seen snow there.

Spring

Winter lingers in Ohio, but one morning the floor of the woods is spread with spring beauty wildflowers. They look white, but are a delicate pink. Then the trillium; purple and yellow violets bloom. We walk to see what else we can find: bloodroot, wild ginger, Jack in the Pulpit, cinquefoil, rue-anemone, and more.

In California the first signs of spring include the spectacular acacia trees blooming brilliant yellow, spewing pollen. The peach orchard is a white wonderland.

Spring meant Easter: new clothes, Easter baskets with jelly beans and yellow marshmallow peeps, trips to see grandparents in Lancaster, and the old man Amos stopping by to plant pansies by the front walk.

We moved into the old farmhouse in April 1961. I drove the moving truck over the lawn to the back steps. The rented truck sank up to the hubcaps in the soft spring mud. The teenager Kelly came with a huge tractor and heavy chain and pulled us out.

Summer

Muggy, humid Philadelphia summers. No air-conditioning, but we had a small electric fan. We made occasional trips to the Fox movie theater downtown because it was cooled. (People who had allergies to ragweed also went there for relief.)

Catching fireflies. Playing in the street till dark.

Summer at the farm meant work. The fields needed mowing every few weeks. The garden needed weeding and deadheading flowers when they faded. Work was best completed in the cool of the morning.

Summer meant weekend visits with friends. T-bone steaks or inch-thick pork chops on the grill with sweet corn on the cob. Or a huge pot of beef stew with potatoes, carrots, and onions, baked for hours in the oven. Gracie Behn made the best potato salad when we had hamburgers made from beef that Luke Swinehart ground for us at the general store that morning.

Summer thunderstorms with torrential rain, lightning, and roaring winds came and went in an hour. Sun on both sides of the downpour.

Fall

Different varieties of maple trees turn yellow, red, or mottled gold. Oaks turn brown. A few weeks later, a high wind comes up, and there is a beautiful, colorful shower of leaves blowing through the woods.

Saturday afternoon means football. As a teenager at Lower Merion High School, I was the football manager, taping ankles, changing cleats when it rained, and moping in a corner if we lost a game. As adults we went to watch Ohio State play where Coach Woody Hayes's teams featured power football with a "cloud of dust." But the OSU band was the best part of the afternoon. If you went early enough, the band played a concert in the field house before going to the stadium.

In California, summer becomes fall quietly, imperceptibly. Deciduous tree leaves turn red, yellow, or brown and fall when the wind blows. Pansies are bedded for the winter, an occasional confused rose or azalea blooms, and the temperature falls to the midfifties.

The season cycle begins again and we grow older.

A DISAPPEARING
DEMOGRAPHIC

Obama won the 2012 election because "the demographics have shifted." Only grumpy old white males voted for Romney. That's me. I fit the waning demographic perfectly. I'm eighty-four, bald, white, Anglo-Saxon, Protestant, retired, irritated, and male. I don't feel like a dinosaur, but I am one. I live in a retirement community, isolated from the great "out there."

My conservative son-in-law is young, but he voted for Romney too. Oh, he is over fifty, white male, Anglo-Saxon, and a little grumpy too. I guess we share a common characteristic. We are a disappearing demographic. We are has-beens, never destined to be in the political mainstream again.

Why did we lose the election so badly? Because Romney was not an effective candidate. He was wooden. He never bantered informally with his audience. When the crowds cheered, he stood and looked this way and that like a robot. It began to annoy me. *Loosen up*, I thought. *Get real. Speak to me.* My wife, usually levelheaded, told me that she voted for Obama. The reason? She didn't trust Romney.

However, I think I am an example of the Republican party of the future. I am by nature quite liberal on social issues. Our founding documents proclaim the right to pursue happiness. Governments should not tell us who can marry who. The right to pursue personal happiness means that government should not legislate what size soft drink we should drink. Do not legislate my behavior that hurts no one else.

The Republican primary debates soiled all the Republican hopefuls. Newt Gingrich had the advantage for a while, but his massive ego and irrationality oozed through. In 2016 I hope the party refuses to participate in those primary flagellations again.

The billions spent by each presidential candidate were largely wasted. The television ads were too negative, and we turned a deaf ear. The telephone calls were fake, automated recordings. (We'd hang up as soon as the "caller" announced him—or herself.) Yes, we guarantee freedom of speech in America, but I won't listen unless that speech is alive and talking to me about things I care about.

So, where are we? Nothing has changed. Partisanship is alive and ugly. Politics is troubling, the government is too intrusive, our national debt is shameful, and old white males are no longer a factor.

Pardon me while I take a nap.

Recollections of Bad Nauheim, Germany

Drafted during the Korean war and eventually sent to Ft. Benning, Georgia, for Infantry Officer Candidate School, I graduated high enough in my class to select my future branch of service. I chose the Medical Service Corps (medical administration). After several months of training at Ft. Sam Houston in Texas, my next assignment in 1952 was to Bad Nauheim, Germany, to run a small health clinic in Butzbach, north of Frankfurt.

Officers were billeted in a massive turn-of-the-century residential hotel, the Kaiserhof. My room on the third floor had a small balcony overlooking the railroad station nearby. The bed was more than comfortable, with a feather mattress and comforters to match. A maid straightened up each day and did my laundry weekly. The only thing missing was a piano and a radio. So I rented an upright piano carried up three flights of stairs and bought a huge Grundig radio bartered for several months of rationed cigarettes. The wash basin was surrounded with elaborately carved marble.

Bad Nauheim is a resort town featuring a spa of delightful Art Nouveau buildings in the center of the old town. A well-known heart clinic is located just beyond the spa, and the major streets featured small clinics where people could recuperate in hotel settings. Nearby was a park where mineral waters sprayed down over towers of twigs where people with lung problems could rest, breathing in the beneficial, fetid air. A few streets near the Lutheran church featured modern shops, selling goods for the tourists, natives, patients, and army soldiers.

My platoon of medics lived in a centuries-old stone castle in Butzbach, a medieval town about five miles north of Bad Nauheim. Our clinic was located in a building adjacent to the castle. We held sick call every morning. Two German doctors treated the soldiers who were authentically ill. (Most were not.) One of the doctors, Hans Sieman, was married and lived near the campus. The other doctor was single and was trying desperately to seduce one of the USO girls to marry him so that he could come to America and become a US citizen.

Several times a year, we would be rousted out of bed in the middle of the night to go to the "field," an exercise to protect the Fulda Gap where the dastardly Russians were expected to invade. We would set up a Battalion Aid Station to care for the wounded. The Russians never invaded, and dying soldiers never arrived. But for the first time in my life, I camped out in a foot of snow, drinking hot coffee to stay warm. Most of the time in the field was spent socializing with friends.

I was assigned a driver, a nice young fellow in an open medic jeep. He picked me up each morning at seven, and I would eat breakfast and lunch at the mess at the castle.

After work I ate dinner at a restaurant in Bad Nauheim. The war had been over for six years, and the restaurants were well stocked with meat, fresh vegetables, and German wines. My culinary education was underway. Most meals began with a small tossed salad with vinaigrette, followed by a plate-sized schnitzel served with fried potatoes and two veggies slathered in butter and kept warm on a searing hot metal plate. The waiter would keep my plate stocked until I hollered, "Stop!" (Did you know that *Schnitzel a la Holstein* is a schnitzel with a fried egg on it?)

I learned to drink wine with my food. Three wines were dominant in that area: Rheingau, Rheinhessen, and Mosel. All were white, slightly sweet, and perfect for long hours of sipping. Like the natives, I would bring a book or newspaper to the restaurant and sit late into the evening sipping wine before returning to the Kaiserhof.

To keep from becoming bored, I took up photography. I bought an Argus C3 at the PX and started shooting in the neighborhood. I learned to develop and print the pictures, and sent them home. USO tours took me to Paris and Italy. I loved classical music and attended the reopening of the restored Frankfurt Opera House that had been destroyed by Allied bombs. On two occasions, I traveled to Bayreuth for the Wagner Festival that had just reopened after the war to hear *Der Meistersinger* and *Parsifal*. I visited the Goethe House in Frankfurt and read *Faust* and *The Sorrows of Young Werther*, which introduced me to an entirely new literary category.

My first commander of the battalion was Col. Wayne Winder. He was bright, handsome, and a West Point graduate. After a year in Butzbach, he was transferred as special liaison to the Russians in East Berlin. He invited me to visit his wife and him in Berlin, where he drove me into the East Sector. The Berlin Wall had not yet been built, and daily visits to the sector were normal. I admit I became uncomfortable when we encountered a flag-waving Communist youth group marching nearby. When Winder left, he was replaced with an overweight, dull colonel who bragged that he was last in his class at West Point.

My crowning achievement in Bad Nauheim was to start a trousseau. I went to a fancy hardware store and bought a set of Rosenthal china of twelve settings. Down the street, I bought a set of delicate stemware, the glass so thin and fragile that every time we used and washed it, something would shatter. Nearby on the Czech border, I ordered a custom set of crimson-and-gold espresso cups that we used until we left our farm home in 1987, when they went to auction.

The mayor of Butzbach wanted the German citizens to use our American tennis courts, and he called a meeting of a team of officers from the base to discuss the matter. The meeting in the medieval city hall began with coffee and cake, and then a citizen described the history of Butzbach during the previous five hundred years. Their long history, they explained, recommended that they be permitted to play tennis on our courts. We turned down their request.

Living in Bad Nauheim was an amazing, eye-opening experience for an inexperienced twenty-one-year-old. Many years later, Marian and I took our friends Steve and Barbara Borik back to relive old times. The town had become surrounded by new construction, which confused me. But arriving in the center of town, it all came back. The Kaiserhof had been turned into an apartment building and the army had abandoned Butzbach, but a few of the old restaurants where I ate each night were still serving crispy wiener schnitzels.

An adage states that all things change, but in this case, not much. My memories have flooded back.

BAD NAUHEIM POSTSCRIPT

Marian and I were walking near the Kurhaus in Bad Nauheim when we passed the place where the waters were doled out to visitors. We entered the beautiful room with polished brass faucets and water streaming out. It reminded me of the gorgeous Pump Room in Bath, England, where the British elite met in season to drink the famous water there.

In the two years I lived in Bad Nauheim, I had never gone into the building. When I used to walk by the place on weekends, I noticed that most of the people going inside were elderly, and many were infirm. The room featured a marble island in the middle of the room, perhaps fifteen feet across and circular, with a dozen or so elaborate brass spigots supervised by several women in starched uniforms. Rows of sparkling glasses in stainless-steel holders awaited customers.

"Wasser, bitte," I requested. The lady poured a few inches into the glasses, and Marian and I tasted the water. It was unpleasant, with a stinky mineral, medicinal taste. We took a few moments to swallow our portion and walked out into the park. We had not gone far when my intestines started to growl and complain. "I think we better get back

to the hotel," I said. We barely made it back before my lower end exploded.

Now I know why the exit from the *kurhaus* had prominent rooms labeled *Dammen* and *Herren* near the entrance and why so many old folks went there every day.

FEAR OF FLYING

Colleague and psychiatrist Hugh Missildine told me that if man were meant to fly, he would have a huge breastbone. The Wright brothers invented a machine we can sit in and fly around the world at thirty thousand feet. It's eerie and miraculous.

Flying is both intriguing and boring. Fly from Columbus, Ohio, to Tokyo, and you will wonder why you bothered. I did that once on the way to the Philippines. (I never longed to fly to Australia because of the excessive distance.)

The first time I flew was in the early 1950s on my way to a job interview. The plane was a DC-3, a vibrating, noisy propeller-driven airplane. For the next fifty years, I flew in larger and larger planes: those beautiful TWA Constellations, then DC-10s, and eventually the gigantic 747s.

Our company traded in a single-engine Beechcraft Bonanza for a twin-engine Bonanza about the time I was hired. It seated six people and was perfect for the short hop to Sturgis, Michigan, where one of our plants was located. Fred Snell was our pilot, and he permitted one passenger to sit in the cockpit, letting us "steer" once in a while. Before taking off, he would arrange a catered tray of sandwiches and munchies. It seemed luxurious, but after we merged with Abbott. It all changed. They bought several large jets seating twelve. They had a hostess, elegant food, a decent restroom, and a locker of booze for the trip home. Fred Snell was retired because he didn't have jet training, and we missed his informality. My travel was sometimes on company planes, but mostly commercial. Unfortunately commercial travel became more Spartan each year, but we were permitted to travel first class if an international flight exceeded five hours.

I never longed to learn to fly. Some of my friends owned private planes. Steve Borik, our human relations vice president, had a summer home on a lake in Michigan. Each weekend, weather permitting, he would fly his Cessna to the lake. His wife, Barbara, drove there the day before with supplies and prepare dinner for Steve when he arrived Friday night. He would buzz their home, land nearby, and his drink would be waiting for him on arrival.

He invited us to share a weekend with them, and I flew with Steve. The cockpit was sun filled heading northwest and the temperature in the cockpit neared eighty degrees. I could barely stay awake. The drone of the motor was soporific, and I couldn't wait for some cool, fresh air. Pilots tell you that flying is 95 percent boredom with a few minutes of terror every once in a while.

During the seventies and eighties, I traveled overseas regularly. I discovered that an Agatha Christie novel exactly filled in the flight between New York and London. Attempts to drink my way across the Atlantic were failures, requiring a full day of recuperation. Finally I learned to go to the hotel after an overseas flight, shower and shave, rest for an hour, and go out for a long sightseeing walk. One business trip required me to circumnavigate the globe. That was exhausting and ruined my desire to fly anywhere.

As the airline industry matured, airports became larger and larger. Some airports erected buildings for individual airlines. At Heathrow in England, a bus would sometimes be required, taking thirty minutes to go a different gate. In Atlanta an automated subway moves you hither and yon. As my back became more distorted, I needed an electric cart to whisk me to a new gate, or occasionally I needed a wheelchair to push me where I needed to go.

During fifty years of travel, the food service became worse and worse. After short-hop meals were discontinued altogether, I once paid eight dollars for a dry and inedible ham and cheese sandwich. Earlier, commercial flying was a treat. A first-class meal was served with linen, fine china, crystal, and roasts carved in the galley. Airline chicken became a national joke. Warm, moist hand towels after meals degenerated into paper towelettes.

After retirement, most of Marian's and my flights were to go to cruise ships sailing from distant ports. Those flights became the low points of the vacation. Like our aging bodies, the airline industry has been steadily disintegrating. Too bad—it was once a treat to buckle up and fly.

But as Hugh Missledine told me, our breastbones are too small to wave our arms and fly off to Chicago. Evolution works too slowly to wait for wings to sprout.

In the meantime, I will stay home and watch travel shows.

Trivia Continued: Jordan Almonds

A fleeting childhood memory prompted me recently to order a bag of Jordan almonds on the Internet. I love them. A popular box of chocolates offered when I was a boy and was sold by the Whitman Chocolate and Confections Company. The Whitman's sampler contained a handful of these almonds. (The Whitman plant was located in the shadow of the bridge from Philadelphia to Camden over the Delaware River.)

In the mid-1930s, the sampler came in a metal box; later, it would come in a cardboard box that was still being produced in 2012. We frequently had a box at home for special occasions, especially at holidays. Everyone in the family had a favorite treat. Mine was the few Jordan almonds in the selection. My parents and brothers understood that the Jordan almonds were mine.

For the uninitiated, a Jordan almond is a whole nut coated in a hard sugar coating. They are tinted in pastel coloring: yellow, green, purple, and white. They are barely flavored with a light vanilla touch. You crack into the hard coating and chew the almond. Not much of a thrill, but enough to want another and another and another and another.

When my brain flings these tidbits of memory into consciousness, I marvel that a little bit of Jordan almond memory is still lurking there.

What other surprises await?

PREDICTING THE FUTURE

All sorts of charlatans have claimed they could predict the future. Many have tried, and most have failed. How many times have crackpots predicted the end of the world? Doomsdays come and go, and we are no worse for wear. Do polls predict people's future behavior? Tom Dewey was sure to beat Harry Truman for the presidency, but Dewey lost. Trying to attach the future to the present is a lost cause. Forget it. Hope is the expectation that one can see better days ahead, only to be disappointed when cancer or bad luck changes the course of a person's future. Or good things can happen. You can win the lottery, buy the right stock, or marry a rich spouse.

The seventies was an era of futurists. The US government set up several well-funded future centers. One was located in Palo Alto at the Stanford Research Institute. Bill Harman and his team imagined a future with successful remote viewing where experts could see lost objects like hikers or submarines, schools where children learned languages by being put in a trance state while foreign languages were whispered in their ears. Engineers went into deep meditation hoping to bring answers about new sources of energy from aliens in outer space. (Seriously.)

Alvin Toffler and his wife wrote popular best sellers, titled *Future Shock* and *The Third Wave*, detailing the new utopias. Peace would reign, and mankind would become harmonized in the new technological age. Their theory said that if we could see the future, we could take actions to get us to that future. Did they describe the iPhone? No, but Dick Tracy did.

The problem is that the future has a mind of its own. It won't behave. As the saying goes, "The best laid plans of mice and men often go astray." Toynbee the historian predicted that the final great war would be between the East and the West. Maybe someday that might happen. In the meantime, we have an unpredicted fatal international war between radical Islamists and the rest of us, including most moderate Muslims. The earth is warming, and no one seems to know exactly why. Is it a man-made crisis, or that the earth has tilted a bit off its axis? Then what? Dire predictions of flooding in New York City haven't yet shut down Broadway. Not to worry. Most meteors have missed us by miles, but a big crash could happen any day.

Optimists claim that science will bail us out. Out of what? The human brain is flush with things like emotion, good and evil thoughts, and philosophies that belie human management.

Are we helpless before the future? Optimists will say no; pessimists will say yes.

Aztec prediction states that gravity will end on December 21, 2012, and we will all float off into space.

Let's have a drink.

SNACKS:
FOOD FOR THOUGHT

Many people in the world get along on one meal a day. In America, we eat three times a day. Is that enough? No. We supplement those meals with something we name "snacks." Many parents give their toddlers a "bedtime snack." My mother made me an eggnog shake: a glass of milk with an egg, a bit of vanilla, and a touch of sugar. She claims it was the only way she could get an egg into me.

But as adults, we now indulge ourselves in snacks. I have Hershey's Kisses by my computer, cashews by the couch. Marian has pretzels and honey-roasted peanuts by her chair. Yesterday we received a new supply of Werther's caramels. We have dried apricots in the pantry and Ritz crackers in the cupboard above the stove. Next to the icebox we keep a box of York Peppermint Patties. No small pang of hunger goes unfulfilled.

We keep Snickers bars in the refrigerator for emergencies (e.g., low blood sugar). Our microwave popcorn supply is depleted and should be on next week's shopping list. The Kettle potato chip supply is also at zero. I order them by the case on the Internet. Our cookie drawer is next to the stove and usually contains a box of Oreo cookies. Our SRC dining room bakes cookies every day. After dinner we may bring home oatmeal raisin, peanut butter, chocolate chip, or snickerdoodle cookies for an emergency hunger.

Do we have any healthy snacks in the house? Yes, we keep apples in the fridge and often some other fruit for cereal. But we rarely eat them between meals.

Do you consider a block of Swiss cheese a potential snack? It could be a snack, but usually we have it with a sliced apple for breakfast when the mood hits us. Are you wondering what kind of weird foodies we have become in our old age? What rationale could possibly explain this gluttony? And what has happened to our weight?

We discovered six months ago that Marian had almost stopped eating. She was losing weight, was sleeping twenty hours a day, and was lethargic when she was awake. Eventually we discovered that she was seriously overmedicated and dehydrated. In time, we were able to reduce the offending medicines, rehydrate her, and give her an appetite stimulant, Megese. Now she is eating heartily, eating regular meals, snacking all day, gaining weight and looking and feeling 100 percent better.

My belt has only lost one notch. Viva la snacks

THE LEFTOVERS

The average life expectancy in the United States was 77.58 years in 2010. Marian and I live in an assisted living facility where nearly everyone is in their eighties, and many are in their nineties. That makes us among those who have beaten the system. Does it mean that we have lived lives during which we have eaten only broccoli, exercised twice a day, never smoked or drank to excess, led a stress-free life, or never argued? No, it meant that we inherited longevity genes from some remote but long-lived ancestor.

We are the societal leftovers who hang around behaving as if our lives are before us. Some among us will still get out on the dance floor to shake a leg, assuming that our knees will still hold us up. Others still have enough energy left to initiate new things, take trips, complain about the food, and lead discussions. But I have noticed that while most of us are pleasant and passive, we easily become aggravated and grumpy if things don't go our way.

Some of us can't remember how old we are. When asked, Ernie raises fingers, first nine fingers and then four fingers—ninety-four. Marie says she doesn't know how old she is, but remembers she was born in 1922, as was

George. When told by her aging children that they were planning a big birthday party in July when Marie turns ninety, she asked, "Am I ninety?"

After repeating the same story for the sixth time, leftovers will note, "I may have told you that." Repetition really doesn't matter. A repeated story has the comfort of a third martini. The punch line is like meeting an old friend.

Bodies become frail, but some still go to the nine a.m. chair exercise class to retain their muscle tone. Many go to the class on their electric scooters or walkers. When the dining room doors open, the parade is mechanized. Staff remove the walkers during meals and return them during dessert, all in the name of decorum.

This is not to disparage we elderly. We've made it to a glorious age, even though "glorious" hardly is an appropriate adjective—rusty is more like it. We wake achy and stiff, gobble pills to keep the pharmaceutical industry profitable, and seek the comfort of pleasant memories.

Because short-term memory fades first, we talk about our youth and childhood. A resident told me that his Methodist upbringing was so strict that he was not allowed to dance, smoke, drink, or have much fun. Even having a pack of cards in the house was a sin. As he repeated the history of his innocent youth, someone reported that he was watching x-rated movies in his room. Okay, we grow up and can change our ways.

Leftovers are considered better the next day: soup, meatloaf, and other comfort foods. Old seniors do have a charming way of approaching things. My way or no way. We don't have time to stand around and argue.

WEATHER:
AN APPRECIATION

Rain and Thunderstorms

In Saratoga, California, rain is a good thing because we don't get much of it. Most of the year, the flowerbeds are watered, and I worry whether the peach orchard nearby will receive enough rain during the rainy season to produce juicy peaches. So far, the winter rain of 2012-2013 has been adequate.

As a small boy, we had a rainy-day ritual. Mother would put up our card table, throw a sheet over it, and invite me to spend the day in my new house. She would bring me a peanut butter and jelly sandwich with a glass of milk at noon. A rainy day was a day of imagination and childhood delight.

Later as an adult, I would go to the new floor-to-ceiling windows during a violent thunderstorm and watch sheets of rain blow across the pond with trees swaying dangerously in the roaring wind.

Snow

What a joyous event whenever the first snow fell each year in Philadelphia. It meant that Christmas was coming, that we could make snowballs, and if it snowed hard enough, that we could construct a snow fort or a snowman. We wore high galoshes with metal buckles, gloves sewn with a long cord passed through our coats so one glove couldn't be lost, and woolen caps with ridiculous pompoms on top. Flexible Flyer sleds came out of the basement, and we'd trudge to the hilly golf course nearby for an afternoon of up and down the hills, specializing in belly flops.

When we lived in the new house on the Ohio farm, the electricity would sometimes go off for a day or so after a snowstorm, and we would live in the living room, heating a pot of snow on the Franklin stove for drinking and flushing toilets. (Melted snow water has a peculiar flavor.) On one occasion, we ran out of firewood, and we called a local farmer, Chuck Shafer, to bring us a new supply. We remained toasty. (Unfortunately Chuck committed suicide when he got into drugs and alcohol. His wife found him hanging in their shed.)

Ice Storms

Ice storms are more dangerous. They usually occurred in early spring when April rain turned to ice, and we became marooned with no power. The woods were spectacular, every branch a gleaming work of art. Sometimes the daffodils were already in bloom and became encased in ice. The trees over our long lane made an archway of white with the threat of a tree or large branch falling, closing off our escape route. And escape we sometimes did, slipping and sliding out to the road. From there a friend would take us into the city where we would be safe in Gil Martinez's apartment.

Summer Heat and Humidity

I was raised long before air-conditioning was common, but my family did own one little ten-inch electric fan. At bedtime, each child was put to bed with the fan one after the other. Later Dad bought a rotating fan, and that was considered a modern marvel. On very hot nights, Dad would take us downtown to a movie theater that advertised that it was air-conditioned. It was a double treat—coolness and a movie. When you exited the theater, the heat and humidity blasted you again.

Summer heat brought fireflies. After dark, Mother would prepare a mayonnaise jar with holes in the lid and send us out into the alley. After capturing a dozen or so lightning bugs, we'd go to bed with the jar glowing intermittently. But in the middle of the night, you would watch pulsating fireflies climbing bedroom walls. I could never understand how they could escape those tiny holes in the lid.

Fog

Once or twice a year, we wake to a pea-soup fog, and I can't see across our courtyard. Real pea soup is opaque, but our pea-soup fog is usually translucent. The fog is lovely but rarely lasts an hour or so.

Another phenomenon warrants mention. We live about twenty miles from the Pacific Ocean, shielded by the Santa Cruz mountains. The coast is cold and foggy most of the time, and as fog blows eastward, it meets the mountains. At times the fog spills over the ridge, and as it descends into our valley, it evaporates and our sky remains clear. Cheap entertainment.

Weather Is Not Funny

For three days, I have been trying to think of something funny to say about weather. I looked up Mark Twain's famous quotation, "Everybody talks about the weather, but nobody does anything about it." Several Internet sites say that he never said or wrote it. Nor did he say, "The coldest winter I ever spent was a summer in San Francisco," according to others. So instead of finding humor, I am in a quandary over whether you can trust traditional adages.

Should we worry about global warming? What if the earth is a bit off its axis? How many decades will it take before it rights itself and all weather becomes normal again?

Maybe I won't sleep well tonight.

WHEN THINGS GO WRONG

As I grow older and wiser (perhaps), I tell people that the fifties are their best years. Why? Because you had already experienced most of the things that can go wrong—some illnesses, an overdrawn bank account, a car crash, a robbery. We weathered those storms, and when more bad things happened, we could remark, "Oh, that again."

Unfortunately things can continue to go bad, and solutions do not look promising. Today, for example, our daughter with an MBA wants to go back to work, but so far no takers. The second daughter with MS is becoming worse. A leg went numb. Her husband, an ICU nurse for twenty-five years, hurt his back lifting a three-hundred-pound patient and is on disability. My wife has some sort of disorder that seems to baffle MDs.

I was recently chosen to chair the Resident Council at Assisted Living in our retirement community. My expectations were high that I might be able to help our residents enjoy their elderly lives a bit more, remain safer, and even have better food. Small chance. What emerged are complaints about spots on rugs, a stolen wallet, and dining room chairs without gliders. I have resigned.

Life will inevitably have as many downs as ups. Bad times are as unstoppable as the rising sun. Some fool called these the "golden years." They're not. They are the downward years, rusty, forgetful, and ominous.

Phooey!

Fear Not to Speaketh the Truth

In an attempt to make you feel sorry for me, I offer this adventure that occurred recently. This is not high art and can be enjoyed only if you are not offended by dirty stories—and I mean *dirty*.

I've had back trouble since the 1980s, when scoliosis started making an s-shape of my degenerating spine. For many years, I managed the discomfort with OTC painkillers plus occasional cortisone shots in my fanny by a physician known as an interventional radiologist.

Eventually I was introduced to a nonaddictive opiate drug named tramadol taking one long-acting pill a day. I spent my late seventies and eighties pain-free. Then one day, I discovered that I didn't need the tramadol and started taking only a Tylenol once a day. Tramadol is a great drug, but here is its dirty little secret: it is constipating, bad enough to require laxatives every other day or so. On Ducolax days, I would avoid any activities outside the apartment.

Eventually, the pain in my knee and back returned, especially in the wee hours of the night. I had an annual physical, and my internist and I had a full discussion of my aching back and that tramadol was not working. He said we should try morphine, and I started two pills a day. The pain disappeared, but by the third day, I became aware that I had not been to stool, so I took some of my adored Ducolax. Nothing. Two more days, more Ducolax, and still nothing. Then on the sixth day, the concrete dam started pressing against the ureter, and urine could not get through. I was in serious trouble.

I sent messages to my internist, the nursing staff, my son-in-law (the intensive care nurse), and my daughter (the nurse anesthetist). Advice started pouring in—stop the morphine, high colonics, Miralax, Fleet enemas, prunes, etc.

Early on the seventh day, I took a very large dose of Ducolax, and the certified nurse assistant brought me a dose of milk of magnesia. At 11:45 that night, the dam broke. The bed was a mess, my drawers were a mess, the bathroom floor was a mess. The deluge lasted half a day before I began to feel normal.

After two days, I restarted morphine again but soon started to seize up. A new regimen was called for. I stopped taking morphine.

For the record, I now practice limited pain management—not too little help, not too much. This modest essay is more about morphine than you may have wanted to know. After I stopped taking morphine everything is back to normal. What's a little pain?

Painkillers were a shitty experience.

LET'S BE HONEST

It makes me mad when someone says, "It's better than the alternative." My fervent wish was once to live out a long life, unlike my brothers and father. Now I have arrived at that long life, and it irritates me that old age brings a lot of downers—nothing unexpected or unusual, mind you, just the usual: achy legs, some loss of short-term memory, death of good friends, and general frailty.

Oh, stop whining. You wanted a long life, worked at it, and now you are stuck with it. So settle down, wimp, it's all very normal. Every sage in history described it. Shakespeare said this in that famous "all the world's a stage" soliloquy from *As You Like It*.

Last scene of all
That ends this strange eventful history
Is second childishness and mere oblivion.
Sans teeth, sans eyes, sans taste, sans everything.

Compensation is a necessity for the elderly. As our limbs fail, we substitute canes, walkers, and then electric scooters that become our working limbs—unless we forget to plug them in.

Dementia is our inevitable fate, but dementia works backward. We remember things that happened when we were ten but not what happened yesterday. My mother had Alzheimer's disease and did not recognize me, but she could sing, "You Are My Sunshine" in harmony, with two verses flawlessly remembered.

Several nights ago, as Marian and I waited for the dining room to open, two ladies began to sing "You Are My Sunshine" in tune and with every word correct. That afternoon the instigator had aimlessly wandered into a friend's room saying she was looking for someone to have fun with.

Mortality is a constant companion, not in a morose way, but as a shadow that cannot be avoided. Of the six people with whom we ate regularly, four are gone. I passed an apartment that was being repainted because its occupant had died. The director of our retirement community walked by, and I said, "There's a lot of turnover recently."

"Well," she said, "It's that time of year." (Meaning flu season, I presume.)

Hell no, I thought, *it's spring, the time of renewal. Think more positively.* New residents appear to replace those who have died; new flowers bloom to replace those who have faded.

George McGreagor said that his worst loss was giving up his car. Marie said the same. Next month I plan to stop driving, another milestone in the seven stages of man.

Don't mope—no more car washes, gas fill-ups, expensive car insurance, nor rent for the parking space. What a savings, but taxi fares might negate the savings. Who knows.

In our dotage, we are left with a subtle and ever-present sense of anger and frustration. When people say, "It's better than the alternative," they are asking for a fight.

Damn it, get real! I'm eighty-four!

PS: My favorite joke about old men: John Glenn went into space when he was seventy-seven. It is reliably reported that he forgot to turn off the left turn signal on his spaceship.

Dad

Dad's funeral was held at the Oliver Bair Funeral Home in downtown Philadelphia, an institution known for burying important citizens. I never knew that Dad was somebody special; he was just Dad, the political editor of the Philadelphia *Evening Public Ledger* who covered the state legislature and local politics. Dad had had his first stroke a year earlier but recovered sufficiently to go back to work, walking with a cane. His second and fatal stroke occurred in the office of Harry Davis, the executive assistant to Joe Pew, who owned the Sun Oil Company (Sunoco). (Pew donated liberally to the Republican Party and was considered a political force.)

When our family arrived at the funeral home for the viewing, we were astounded to find three large rooms filled with flowers floor to ceiling and dozens of strangers milling around the casket. Mother and my brothers were seated off to the side, and a flow of people stopped by to tell Mother that Dad had done them a favor—helped to find a new job, gave a ten-dollar loan when broke, helped to get a kid into college. What a wonderful person he had been, they reported. That night he was exalted, and it came as a surprise.

As I grew to maturity, I began to search for the father others knew. He died when he was forty-one. His parents lived to old age, so it wasn't genetics. Slowly I began to realize that he was in the hard-drinking, chain-smoking, fedora-wearing role of the 1930s newspaper reporter depicted in novels and in the theater. I never saw him drunk, but at home he drank warm gin from a jelly glass. He chain-smoked and rolled tobacco from the ends of his cigarettes so that when he lit them they would flare with fire. He liked a hot smoke. He loved to have people around him, and someone was usually visiting for a drink or staying overnight. He was an enthusiastic host and had a devilish, twinkling sense of humor. He paced.

He always drove too fast and was often stopped for speeding. He had been given an honorary sheriff's badge by Aus Meehan, the elected sheriff in Philadelphia. Dad pinned the impressive badge to his wallet and flashed it when pulled over.

Dad was away often, particularly when the state legislature was in session in Harrisburg. He would drive there Sunday night and return home on Friday. I can imagine him playing poker and drinking with his cronies throughout the week. He loved to gamble and play the horses. Whether he ever cheated on Mother I will never know, but it wouldn't surprise me if he had. (Once when Marian and I visited my demented mother, she looked at Marian and spat out, "I hate that woman." One of Dad's brothers married a shady lady.)

Dad typed furiously with two fingers. Our family was seated in the balcony of the Philadelphia convention center when Wendell Willkie was nominated for the presidency in 1940. I remember looking down at the press box to see Dad, fedora cocked on his head, typing his story as fast as his two fingers could manage. He went on the Willkie campaign trail and returned with all his metal pin-on credentials for us to wear and play with. On election night, we sat by the big Philco radio in the living room to record returns.

As a father, he was perfect, loving, and interested in doing things with my brothers and me. He was so proud of the twins, Jack and Jim, and would never miss a high school football game when they played. He took me deep sea fishing and taught me to fly cast before taking me to fish for trout. When I was five or six, he bought me a little gift on his way home from work every day. Sometimes it was just two Chiclets bought from a penny gum machine. On payday he would stop at the toy store at the station and buy something a little more substantial.

In 1939 he and Mother bought a lovely fieldstone home in the suburbs where he planted roses, his favorite flower, in the deep shade in the backyard. He over-fertilized the grass in the front yard, and we had ugly dead spots for a season. Domesticated he was not.

He loved to hunt with his brothers in the fall. He was especially proud of his double-barreled shotgun. They hunted pheasants and rabbits. Mother had no interest in cooking the kill, so Dad brought home rabbit tails and beautiful feathers for us to examine and display in our bedrooms.

My older brothers, the twins, died of cardiac-related problems in their early forties, as Dad had. Maybe it was genetics after all.

Mother never remarried or even thought about it. She told me that she could never find a husband as wonderful as Dad had been. He died when I was eleven. He would have been an interesting guy to know when I became an adult.

I still wonder about him.

MOTHER

When mother died a few weeks before her ninetieth birthday, I talked with her gerontologist, who reported, "She was a tough lady." Her life was tough.

Mother married and bore three boys, the twins and Tommy. Dad died when she was forty-two, and she raised the boys as a widow. She worked at various jobs, the longest as a dress saleslady at Strawbridge and Clothier, where she was able to buy clothes at a discount. She was always well dressed. Her personality was gentle, kind, and charming. She graduated from high school but never went to college. She read best sellers, did crossword puzzles every day, and loved Bette Davis movies. She sang with a sweet soprano voice.

When I was a child, she smoked Sir Walter Raleigh cigarettes because they had a coupon on the back that she redeemed for glassware. While Dad was alive, she was a typical 1930s housewife, cooking, doing laundry by hand, ironing, and cleaning, especially in spring and fall, when the woodwork was scrubbed and curtains taken down and washed. Rugs were vacuumed with an Electrolux and later an upright Hoover, bought on "time." She rarely raised her voice to correct errant children. She made many of my clothes.

When I went to elementary school, I came home for lunch at noon, and she would have Campbell's tomato soup and a sandwich ready. Her cooking skills were marginal, but she made a delicious pot roast and breaded veal cutlets. She never baked pies, but baked a cake several times a week.

At the end of World War II, my brothers volunteered for the Air Corps. Mother and I developed a new relationship. I became her escort and friend. I called her "pal." We spent our lives together all the time. We played canasta and pinochle with neighbors, went to movies together, shopped together, and went to church together. I was her best friend and protector. When the neighborhood had robberies, I piled glass milk bottles at the doors so we would be warned about an intruder.

As a teenager seeking maturity and freedom, I began to feel uneasy that we were too close, and later asked a psychiatrist whether I had any serious oedipal issues. He told me no, Mother had taught me how to love women.

I lived at home until I was drafted. Jack and Jim were discharged from the Air Corps and started college, living at home. When they married, Mother was alone again. When discharged I moved to Columbus, Ohio. One of the twins' friends built an apartment building in Ardmore and provided Mother a small apartment at a low monthly rent. Her assets were primarily the proceeds from the sale of the fieldstone house she and Dad bought in 1939.

Jim's widow, Minnie, picked her up on Sunday nights for dinner. Contact with me was infrequent, although Marian and I flew her to Columbus each year, and once flew her to Europe to share a trip we had taken to Israel. Her sister, Arlene, took her as a companion to Cocoa Beach, Florida, every winter. She went to Bermuda with her sister once. She worked selling dresses until she was seventy-five.

Eventually, we started noticing personality changes. On one occasion, she called me five times at the office in one day, unaware we had talked earlier. On a visit to Columbus, she started to complain about her daughters-in-law, a behavior that was uncharacteristic. Minnie reported that Mom was spending a lot of time sitting alone in the lobby of her apartment. Mother's brother, Bob, who did her taxes, also noted the changes. He and Minnie contacted me and said, "You have to do something about Edythe." I flew to Philadelphia to take her for a medical assessment. An MRI revealed a tangled brain, and an Alzheimer's diagnosis was confirmed.

We moved her to Westminster Terrace, an assisted living facility in Columbus, where she continued to deteriorate. I stopped by to see her most nights after work. Eventually she didn't recognize me or thought I was her husband. She became agitated if we left her room. Marian and I felt helpless. When she ran out of money, a social worker helped us apply for Medicaid. Mom fell and broke her hip but walked again two weeks after returning from the hospital.

Her first grandchild, Libby, could not say "grandmother" and called her Ginga. All thirteen grandchildren called her Ginga. Mother had a charm bracelet made with the name of each grandchild inscribed on it.

She was a tough lady, as her doctor told me. She weathered grim storms and had some happiness and a lot of loneliness and sorrow, especially when the twins died in their forties. Before becoming demented, she was a charming companion. Her best days were when Dad was alive and she was raising her three little boys.

INSANITY:
IMPERSONAL WARFARE

Sometime in the early 1970s, I had dinner with Roald Campbell, a well-known professor of leadership development at the School of Education of the University of Chicago. He was a longtime innovator, mentor to dozens of school superintendents, author of many books on school reform, and instigator of organizations dedicated to school improvement through innovative experiments.

I was a fellow in the National Program for Educational Leadership and had landed a job supervising a new long-range plan for the Palo Alto Unified School District, so I was deemed worthy of a few hours alone with the great man. Most of our dinner conversation was unexceptional. As we finished our last sip of coffee, I asked, "Roald, what do you worry about?"

Without a moment's hesitation he answered, "Lasers."

He said that technology was developing so rapidly that lasers could target something worlds away with no face-to-face human contact. Warfare had become even more dehumanized. Direct confrontation with an enemy was no longer required.

If you were a Roman slave on a team of gladiators scheduled to fight to the death on Saturday in the coliseum, you would know that your win or loss was in your hands. If you were a Confederate soldier the night before a battle, you could hear the enemy singing songs at their campfires, waiting for early light. If you were a pilot in World War I, you might wave at the Red Baron as his plane flew by before you looped and trained your machine gun on him. Warfare was personal and often one-on-one.

The Chinese invented gunpowder, enabling combatants to be at great distances from one another. Now we can attack without being anywhere near the enemy. Satellites can see everywhere around the globe from a bunker in Maryland.

We are currently having a national debate on the future of unmanned drones and our military's ability to pinpoint and blow up a small house a half continent away, all with GPS systems and laser-guided armory. No more hand-to-hand combat to train for, just mastery of a software program.

Dozens of new policy and pragmatic implications arise: national borders no longer matter. How can we validate collateral human damage? How is verification of damage documented? What is the future role of foot soldiers? What is the future of impersonal warfare?

For example, when we planned to invade Japan at the end of World War II, Harry Truman asked for an assessment of how many soldiers would die if we invaded Japan. The answer was 150,000 American soldiers killed. Truman opted to drop the atomic bomb on Hiroshima and a week later on Nagasaki. The war was quickly ended, and no American soldiers were lost.

Protesters demand humane warfare. Insanity. What is the definition of "humane warfare?" Will special ops take the place of vast armies? (Murder the leadership and spare the masses. That's an old-fashioned idea.) Will we deploy our unmanned drones from TV screens in a building in the pines of New Jersey? Can we justify a preemptive strike?

I am antiwar unless we have been violated. Let us live with the principal of mutual respect.

I am becoming silly and depressed.

Let's hold a high-level weeklong seminar to define humane warfare, in Las Vegas of course, with dozens of highly paid consultants, role-playing generals, and senators, but with time off to play the slots—at taxpayer expense, of course.

WINE:
HERE'S MORE

A bottle of wine never graced my childhood home. Mother and Dad drank mixed drinks for recreation, and wine was never served with meals. I approached adulthood with absolutely no knowledge of wines. The only wines that were advertised in Philadelphia in the thirties and forties were Mogen David and Manischewitz, sweet kosher table wines made from concord grapes.

In college I learned about cheap Chianti because of the bottle it came in, wrapped in straw and used as a candleholder at fraternity parties. But I never drank any Chianti. The frat brothers drank beer.

In the early 1970s, we moved to Palo Alto, California, and my wine education began. Within a few months, we traveled to the Napa Valley to stop at a few wineries for tasting. The first was the Heitz Winery, where Joe Heitz built a small, unpretentious cinderblock tasting room on Route 29 near St. Helena. Heitz was known for creating hearty cabernet sauvignons, and we bought a few bottles for twelve dollars a bottle to serve when we had dinner guests. When we did, I didn't like the cabernet. It was much too big and overwhelmed the food. Heitz also bottled a grignolino rose that we did like, and we often went back to Napa to buy more.

Over the next few years, we got to know Napa better and most of the major wineries there. (In the seventies, there may have been only thirty or so important wineries.) Another favorite was Stag's Leap on the Silverado Trail. We were delighted to learn that Ronald Reagan served Stag's Leap wines to Queen Elizabeth when she visited the White House, and we were drinking it too.

In addition to wineries in the Napa Valley, we frequented a winery in south San Jose, Mirassou, which bottled a slightly sweet Chenin Blanc. We loved that chilled white wine for breakfast when we had guests and Marian made pancakes with sweetened whipped cream and crushed fresh strawberry topping.

We never became rabid about wine, nor did we drink it every day. We saved it for entertaining. Therefore, wine took on an aura of being something special. We learned about the common types of wine and drank some of each, but our knowledge was never sophisticated enough to describe "nose" or the subtle flavors reported in magazines. We subscribed to *Wine Spectator*, but it presented more information than we wanted to know. If a wine rated ninety or more, it became too expensive for us to buy. I never learned much about French wines.

When we returned to California in 2005, we visited the David Bruce winery in the Santa Cruz mountains. Dr. Bruce made excellent pinot noirs that we bought by the case. Another winery we visited nearby was Ridge, famous for their award-winning zinfandels. I had learned about Ridge in the seventies, when it was owned by some engineers from the Stanford Research Institute (SRI). Ridge is no longer owned by the engineers, but the quality of their "zins" has continued to excel. Their tasting room sits on a mountaintop overlooking the Bay Area in a spectacular setting, up a narrow winding road from Saratoga.

I have tasted Chateau d'Yquem twice, perhaps the world's most famous and most expensive sauterne. (A bottle of a current vintage costs $250.) While visiting our advertising agency in New York in the sixties, Artie Sackler, president of the agency, bought us a bottle after dinner one evening. A common legend about the wine is that each grape is picked individually as the "noble rot" sets in, concentrating the sugars. On my retirement as Chair of the Board of the Red Cross in Columbus, the staff bought me a bottle. We drank that sauterne at our fiftieth wedding anniversary. The famous wine is an acquired taste; it is very sweet and viscous, almost oily.

In the 1960s, a PhD in the Columbus R&D department where I worked fancied himself a gourmand. Each year he made wines at home. His sparkling apple wine was bright and refreshing. His other wines were mediocre. Once I volunteered to help him make the next year's wine. I contributed $200 to buy grapes. We flew some zinfandel grapes from California and traveled to southern Ohio to buy some red and white grapes to make other varietals.

His wine was made in huge carboys, which are very large glass jugs. Every once in a while, the heavy jugs needed to be moved for processing. I was traveling around the world at the time, and I seemed to be absent every time the heavy lifting was needed. Finally he said that he wanted to buy me out, and my career as a winemaker was over. He resigned from the company soon after, and I never tasted the zinfandel that we made.

Now that I am eighty-four, I no longer drink. After drinking a whole glass of wine, I begin to feel woozy and disoriented. But wine drinking is a phase everyone should go through.

Cheers! Bottoms up!

COOKING WITH JULIA CHILD

In the early seventies, we purchased a copy of *Mastering the Art of French Cooking* by Julia Child and Simone Beck. It was all the rage and considered *the* cookbook about French cuisine. Because Marian worked every other weekend at Stanford Hospital, I started cooking for the family. My culinary experiments came from this famous book, and a few dishes were delicious, especially chicken supremes—breasts roasted in a pound of melted butter and smothered with reduced heavy cream with a hint of nutmeg.

Julia was becoming a famous TV star, and we watched every program hoping to learn some new technique, but also hoping for an on-set catastrophe to amuse us. Her voice could etch glass, and we were always entertained.

As Julia became more famous, more of her biography became known. We knew that she married an older man whom she met while serving in the OSS in Ceylon. He managed her TV career but lived in her shadow. We didn't realize she was six-foot-three and came from a wealthy, proper, conservative California family. Her father was an ogre.

Now comes a new biography, *Dearie* by Bob Spitz, which reveals most of the facts that shaped her career. She and her civil servant husband Paul were stationed in France, Germany, and Norway, where they absorbed the local food flavors and cooking methods.

The most interesting part of this new biography describes the many years of frustration writing *Mastering the Art of French Cooking*. Julia wanted recipes to be precise and thoroughly tested. Beck wanted a pinch of this or that. The authors fought like tigers and had an intense love-hate relationship.

The saddest part of the book describes husband Paul's slow descent into dementia and frailty. He was a skilled painter whose paintings started degenerating, and his behavior became unpredictable and embarrassing. Even into her eighties, Julia had enormous energy and ambition and was always looking for the next challenge—a new book, a new television series, a new way to promote French cuisine.

But here's the biggest shock of all: she loved hot dogs.

Honest and Unelectable Abe

Abraham Lincoln would never have been elected president in 2012. Gangly, unattractive, with a high-pitched voice, self-educated, frumpy, and a hick from rural Kentucky and Illinois, Lincoln had none of today's groomed-hair candidates' sophistication. His nomination for the presidency was a political compromise.

My appreciation of Lincoln began sixty years ago, when I read Carl Sandburg's multivolume biography, including *The Prairie Years* and *The War Years*. Sandburg's book is a brilliant love letter to the man he most admired. Read these books and you will forever understand why Abe is revered. The tome is prose, but is it poetic. It is unbelievably detailed. Lincoln comes alive.

Lincoln mastered the English language by himself. The many volumes of his writing and speeches leave you wondering how he could have possibly conquered the skills of phrase-making, insightful observation, and lyricism that distinguish his prose. Historians say it is because he read and reread Shakespeare and the Bible, but he also devoured Victorian prose and the high-minded journalism of the time. He could turn a phrase as gracefully as Mark Twain.

Implausibly, the Internet reports that sixteen thousand books have been written about Lincoln. Why? Because he saved our country, significantly helped to abolish slavery in the United States, but also because he was unusual (even peculiar) in so many ways: self-deprecating, moody, funny, friendly, brilliant though unschooled, both realistic and idealistic, down to earth, even bawdy when telling jokes. His is the unbelievable narrative of a man who emerged from poverty and was elected to the presidency.

Even today more new books are being written. Doris Kearns Goodwin published *A Team of Rivals* in 2010, illustrating that his war cabinet was composed primarily of his political rivals. Over time I have read more than a half dozen of those sixteen thousand books, and I am always surprised by new revelations.

Then one night fifty years ago, I woke in the middle of the night with an urge to paint Lincoln's portrait. I located a piece of artist's board about three feet long and a foot wide and my oil paints, and I sat down to start. For some unknown reason, I decided not to use brushes, but to do the portrait from memory using my fingers, some Kleenex, and only red, white, and blue paint. In an hour I was done. After letting the painting dry, I built a frame from some old molding that was lying around and hung it in the house. My daughter has it now.

Lincoln reminds us that a melancholy outsider, even if unusual in so many ways, may become the one who leads us in new directions. We may never understand him fully.

MAGAZINES

Magazines are adult comic books. Through the years, we have purchased subscriptions to dozens of them. The *New Yorker* and *New York Magazine* are favorites. When the *New Yorker* arrives, the first pass is to scan the cartoons. The *New Yorker*'s first editor, Harold Ross, considered cartoons art, but I never did. They are entertaining, and most are funny. (Others are predictable but memorable.) A favorite cartoon has a psychiatrist talking to a couched patient. The caption reads, "But you are inferior."

The second reading of the *New Yorker* focuses on the cartoon contest on the inside back cover. The magazine publishes a cartoon without a caption, and readers submit a caption. Most weeks I submit a caption, hoping that my entry will be the funniest punch line selected. So far no luck. After entering the contest, I check the table of contents to decide if any of the articles are of interest. Nearly every issue has something fascinating to savor.

New York Magazine, another favorite, is less arty and provides a current review of popular culture and the newest fads and restaurant trends in New York.

A short list of our recent magazine subscriptions:

- *Consumer Reports*
- *Architectural Digest*
- *Archaeology*
- *Biblical Archaeology Review*
- *National Geographic*
- *Time*
- *New Yorker*
- *New York Magazine*
- *Smithsonian*
- *British Heritage*
- *In Britain*
- *The Art Newspaper*
- *The Paris Review*

Each magazine has a core of material in which Marian or I have a special interest. Typically we kept a subscription for several years before letting it lapse, then missing it and resubscribing several years later. We are magazine junkies. We can't help ourselves. Magazines are as addictive as potato chips.

My parents subscribed to many magazines. Two are memorable, *Life* magazine and *Coronet*. *Coronet* is the less well known. It was published from 1936 to 1971, an upscale publication with articles and a section dedicated to fine photography. Those photos attracted me as a nine-year-old because female nudes were often included. I recall other magazines at home: *Liberty, Saturday Evening Post, Colliers,* and *Look.* As a teenager, I enjoyed the *Saturday Review of Literature.* The famous *Reader's Digest* reprinted thousands of articles from other magazines. Copies could be found in every dentist's office.

Like newspapers, magazines are disposable, to be scanned, enjoyed, and tossed. In libraries they are deemed periodicals, signifying "occasional." Many general magazines are failing in the 2000s because readers can find news and opinion faster on the Internet. The magazines that are succeeding focus narrowly on one topic, like photography, travel, or stamp collecting.

Unlike magazines, I can't renew my age.

THE GOD PARTICLE

Physicists have isolated the tiny particle that explains mass and hence the knowledge they require to understand both the cosmology of the universe and subatomic activity. In 2012 the gigantic particle collider in Switzerland (CERN) announced they had probably isolated and identified the Higgs boson, the elusive particle hypothesized to explain mass.

I have absolutely no idea what I am talking about, but while resting in a hospital bed in the middle of the night recently, I wondered what would happen if we had to start the universe all over, before the Big Bang.

Things are too complex and need to be simplified. How many distinct universes do we really need? How many subatomic particles, including quarks and leptons, do we need? How many chemicals do we need in the periodic table? How many species of animals do we need to inhabit the earth? How many sentient humans are right for the space we have inherited?

If, as scientists believe, there is a unified theory of everything, how can we account for evolution, that creeping change that keeps proceeding through time? First bacteria, then slime, then amoeba, and eventually complex man with his opposable thumb and forefinger. Do subatomic particles evolve too? Most physicists don't think so. I'm confused.

What a mess man is making of it. When we developed a sense of awe about our world, we started thinking that we required an explanation for everything and started inventing omnipotent gods, dozens of them, followed by a belief in monotheism—many monotheisms in competition with one another, all sure their God is the one and only true one. Throughout history it was often ugly out there. If physicists do figure out a unified theory, then what?

Start over? Won't happen, but we wonder at the complexity of it all. And remember, like other subatomic particles, the Higgs boson doesn't spin, but the world turns . . . on and on and on.

I feel dizzy.

Start Over Again,
Mr. Sisyphus

Pianist Vladimir Horowitz said that if he didn't practice for one day, he knew it. If he didn't practice for two days, his wife knew it. If he didn't practice for three days, the world knew it. Sisyphus was the ancient king of Corinth, condemned for eternity to push a boulder up a hill, only to have it roll down to start over. We are condemned to start over many things in life. Piano playing is one of them. If you don't practice every day, you revert to playing scales again to restore your agility, musicality, and confidence. Each of us has had some big and little rocks to push up hills over and over again. It is frustrating and absurd.

For many years, I used a paper and pencil to earn my living, until the day that the president of the company announced that we would all have desktop computers and type our own draft material. The first computer was a Wang, a company now defunct. It took me several months to master the word-processing program, complicated by the fact that I had never learned to type. Soon, however, the Wang was traded for an IBM, and a second word-processing system required learning a new program. Then I decided to buy a home computer, and I selected an Apple that friends told me was user-friendly, but required learning a third word-processing system. I felt like Sisyphus pushing that damn rock up the hill again.

So too has been my experience with internists who keep me alive. The doctor who diagnosed my diabetes retired, and I searched for a new internist. I asked a business associate, Dr. Ollie Hosterman, who he would recommend. "I don't care about bedside manner. I just want the smartest, most competent internist in Columbus."

Without hesitation he said, "Diane Tallo."

Diane was teaching internal medicine at Ohio State Medical School but just starting a private practice. I may have been her first private patient, or close to it. I explained my family history to her (father and brothers died early), and she said, "You will be my challenge to get you to old age." She was my internist for twenty-five years, and she kept me alive in spite of open-heart surgery, a stroke, and a pacemaker.

In the early seventies, we moved to Palo Alto to work in the school system. I found an internist associated with Stanford. Basically he followed the same procedures and drugs that Diane had established, and I had no health crisis during that period.

When we moved to California again in 2005, the search for a new internist was on, and I was pushing that rock up the hill again. My daughter (the nurse) had worked at the Palo Alto Medical Foundation briefly and recommended

Dr. Barry Eisenberg. Once again I described my family history.

"Since I'm seventy-five, your job is to keep me alive for five more years," I said.

He responded, "Let's go for ten."

I was his patient for seven years, until I stopped driving and began yet another search for a new internist who was closer. The foundation had opened a satellite branch in Los Gatos, and a transfer there would keep me on the same computer system where my records are stored. Barry recommended Dr. Stuart Menaker in that office.

Another day, another rock, another new internist. Frankly, I'm tired of the same old story. I am eighty-four, and my old history is no longer relevant. I am now an old man. Those internists got me to old age. I understand that my mother's genes had more longevity in them than Dad's. She lived until she was ninety, so I may too. With any luck, no more new internists will be needed, no more rocks to push up that doctor hill.

So, Mr. Sisyphus, I am too old to bother pushing rocks around anymore. I would rather take a nap.

AFTERWORD

The theme of this book is *friends*, those wonderful people who add a bouquet of flowers to life. Just because I haven't named you specifically as a friend, it does not mean that you are not now nor ever have been one. Dozens of friends have made my life richer, interesting, and informed. Some friends have skills I long to have, like the ability to draw or sing, or fix a lawn mower, or carve a bird, or play a decent game of golf. Many friends astound me with their unique skills and their friendship. Staying in touch by e-mail is one of each day's pleasures.

No more promises that I am through publishing books. If I can think and type, you may see more, but maybe not. Who knows? Now eighty-four, I don't plan too far ahead. A few weeks ago, I started spitting up blobs of blood, and they called 911 for the squad to transport me to the hospital. The diagnosis was a tracheal ulcer, now healed. As I have noted several times, I value routine and the beauty of a dull, unexciting life. Occasional fog or a brief drizzle is as exciting as I want life to get.

Writing keeps me occupied when I am not reading, napping, or going to meals. Exercise is the work of the devil, and I do not indulge. The place where we live offers dozens of activities every day. I hate to leave our apartment and would rather turn on some classical music and snooze. Why go out and get stimulated and maybe have a bad dream?

May all your dreams be pleasant dreams and your life bearable.